SMART. SAVVY. SUPERSTAR.

Jamie-Lynn Sigler

WISE GIRL

"She is one of the most optimistic and determined young women in the entertainment industry today."

—Lance Bass, *NSYNC

"I wish more young stars were like Jamie-Lynn Sigler—honest, inspiring and extremely down-to-earth....I can't wait to see what she's going to do next."

—*Teen People*

"Jamie-Lynn Sigler is a courageous, inspiring woman. As one of the most successful Latinas in entertainment, she has used her position and fame to help young girls of every nationality and race. She has gracefully embraced her culture and her success, and she has spoken bravely and honestly about her personal struggles. She is a terrific role model not only for Latinas but for all young women."

—*Latina*

JAMIE-LYNN SIGLER

AND SHERYL BERK

WHAT I'VE LEARNED ABOUT LIFE, LOVE, AND LOSS

WISE GIRL

POCKET BOOKS

New York London Toronto Sydney Singapore

An *Original* Publication of POCKET BOOKS

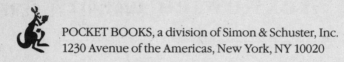

POCKET BOOKS, a division of Simon & Schuster, Inc.
1230 Avenue of the Americas, New York, NY 10020

ISBN: 0-7434-5324-7

First Pocket Books trade paperback printing September 2002

10   9   8   7   6   5   4   3   2   1

POCKET and colophon are registered trademarks of
Simon & Schuster, Inc.

Cover of *Maxim* magazine © Dennis Publishing, Inc.
Photo on cover of *Maxim* magazine © Antoine Verglas

For information regarding special discounts for bulk purchases,
please contact Simon & Schuster Special Sales at 1-800-456-6798 or
business@simonandschuster.com

Printed in the U.S.A.

All photos are courtesy of the author and her agent, Randi Evans.

Acknowledgments

First and foremost, I want to thank **God** for blessing me with the good and the bad and all the in-between. For giving me the strength to get through it, to learn from every experience. I realize that everything I have been through is what shaped me into the person I am today . . . **Mom and Dad:** For your guidance, your love, your patience, and for being my best friends. For taking me through those ups and downs and holding my hand every step of the way . . . **Brian and Adam:** For putting me in your movies, letting me hang with you, and watching over me throughout our childhood and today. You'll always be cooler than me, and our times together are irreplaceable. I love you . . . **Mima and Grandma:** *Te quiero mucho! Numero uno, mi abuela.* I love you to pieces, Gam!!! . . . **Sigler/Lopez family:** For always believing in me and loving me no matter what. And for being a phenomenal extension to a supporting and loving family . . . **To A.J.:** "My hero." For showing me the way. For showing me what a good person really is. For showing me the person I want to be. And for showing me true love. No one has ever gotten through to me the way you have, and no one ever will. B.F.L.C.— M.Y.L.Y. XOXO . . . **All my friends:** For being there, cheering from the beginning, and never forgetting the girl you grew up with. You always make me feel at home. You're the greatest, and I love you all. . . . **Randi:** What would Sheryl and I do without you? You're an organizational genius! . . . **Kerri:** Pubi! I love you. You are number 1, I mean it. . . . **To my entire *Sopranos* family,** for all your love and support. Thank you for the greatest experience of my life . . . **To my HBO family,** especially Angela, Natalie, and Tobe. You always go above and beyond, and I so appreciate it. . . . **Everyone at Pocket Books,** especially Lauren and Louise: For giving me the this incredible opportunity, both to write this book and to work with all of you . . . **Frank:** Thanks for believing this story could reach people as it did you. You owe A.J. and me a drink—that was the most meetings I've ever been to in one day! . . . **Sheryl:** Thank you for all your patience, your effort, your constant belief in the truth and not the fluff. You are an amazing woman with incredible strength. It was a pleasure. If this book helps just one person . . . we win!

Contents

WISE GIRL

Introduction

So there I was on top of the world: starring on *The Sopranos*, appearing on magazine covers and talk shows, making my Broadway debut, releasing a record, rubbing elbows with the rich and famous on the red carpet. "Jamie, you are *so* lucky," people would tell me. And you know what? I felt pretty lucky. I remember thinking, "This can't be real. This can't be happening to *me*, Jamie-Lynn Sigler from Long Island. It must be a dream."

Well, I guess I spoke too soon, because the dream became a nightmare. Just as my career was soaring, my personal life came crashing down around me and I had to pick up the pieces. At twenty-one years old, I've probably seen and experienced more than most people twice my age. Why me? I've asked myself that a lot. Why did I almost starve and exercise myself to death? Why did I let other people's opinions shatter my self-esteem? Why was I suddenly left paralyzed by a disease that no doctors could diagnose?

But I also asked that question during the good times: Why was I chosen—out of dozens of girls—to play Meadow on *The Sopranos?* Why have I been so fortunate in my acting and singing career? Why am I blessed with friends and family who stick by me, no matter what?

Now I'm asking "Why me?" when it comes to writing this book (and maybe you're asking, "So why *her?*"). That's a little easier to answer (all of the above I'll tackle in the upcoming chapters, I promise). Everybody knows me as Meadow Soprano, but there's a real girl behind that character. And trust me, at times, my real life has been just as dramatic (if not more so) than any TV show. I have stories and advice you might want or even *need* to hear. Which doesn't mean I'm going to lecture you like a teacher or a parent, because that's just not me. But I do enjoy sharing my life and I always have a lot to say. My best friends will vouch for me on this—I never shut up.

I'm going to tell you the way I see things now, having survived high school, heartache (and you thought Meadow had problems with Jackie, Jr.?), even life-threatening illness. I've made mistakes, and that's okay. Mistakes are only a bad thing if you fail to learn something about yourself and the world in the process.

As I write this book and relive my experiences, I can

see that I'm not the same person I was three years ago. When I watch the first-season episodes of *The Sopranos,* I think, "Who *is* that girl?" I was so wide-eyed and naive back then. Now, I'm a stronger person, and I'd like to think I'm smarter, too. I'm not talking 1600s-on-the-SATs smart, I'm talking life-smart. I was thrust into an adult world at a very young age—I've been performing since I was eight. Maybe all I've been through has taught me to appreciate things more—simple things, like sharing quesadillas on the set with my "mom" Edie Falco, or hanging out on Christmas break with my best buddies and laughing at each other's dumb jokes. There isn't a day that goes by that I'm not grateful for all that I have and all that I'm doing. But beyond the success, I've also been given this great gift: As an entertainer, I get to reach people and maybe, just maybe, make a difference in their lives.

So why me? Well, why *not* me? I'm not all that different from you, except that I now know some pretty important things that they don't teach you in school. I hope you'll laugh, learn, and maybe even cry a little when you read my book. Or at the very least, say, "Wow! I never knew that about Meadow!" I'll do my best to tell it like it is and it was.

Jamie

1

You Gotta Start Somewhere

I don't have the makings of some legendary Hollywood success story—probably not even a TV movie of the week. I just was this regular kid, growing up in Jericho, New York, in a modest split-level home in a neighborhood called West Birchwood. I had the smallest bedroom and the smallest closet and two older brothers, Adam and Brian, who never let me forget I was the only girl. They teased me mercilessly and always hogged the bathroom we shared.

Not too much happened in Jericho. Probably the biggest excitement was when I was ten, and we built a pool in our backyard (it became the place for most of my birthday parties from then on). I had a lot of friends that lived in my neighborhood, and whenever it was nice weather, we would ride our bikes, swim, and of course play the occasional *pathetic* game of spin the bottle in the school yard. Why "pathetic," you may ask? Well, rather than kiss ("Ewww!"), we would hug. I know, "Jamie, what were you thinking?"

Anyway, aside from the lack of lip-locking in my early years, I had a great childhood. I believe that a lot of who you are as an adult depends on how you're raised—it colors the way you grow to see the world and your place in it. I have an amazing family who inspire me constantly, both through their words and their actions. We're quite a group, us Siglers. Maybe a little stubborn, but always determined, passionate, and resilient. My dad, Steve, was an accountant at a stationary company, but he always felt that he should have been doing something else. He *loved* baseball all through his childhood and adulthood, but between work and the fact that on Long Island there were only softball leagues for him to participate in, his dreams of playing got put on the back burner.

Then one day in 1986, he decided to place an ad in our local paper to get some guys together to play baseball (or as he called it, "hardball") on the weekends. He got a lot of responses, and the next thing he knew, he was spending all his time organizing teams and leagues and games. Of course, he needed help with all this, and whom did he turn to? His family: My mom, Consuelo Lopez (or just plain Connie), who was a full-time mom, became his full-time secretary, and at night, all five of us would set up an assembly line to pack envelopes with info for the guys in the league.

Well, to make a *long* story short, Dad's little hobby turned into quite a business: He now owns the largest amateur baseball league in the world. He has international teams and even a World Series every year. This was what I grew up around: watching my father follow his dreams and turn them into reality. For so long, he worked two jobs, never sleeping, never relaxing, all because he wanted something so badly. My mom is also such a strong lady: She struggled so much as a child, escaping from Cuba as a teenager, not knowing English, not having any money, and without a friend in the world. When my grandmother escaped as well and joined her, they worked day and night just to put food on the table. Yet they never got discouraged—they had faith that God had a plan for them.

I Dreamed a Dream

So with that kind of family history, is it any wonder then that this funny little kid from Jericho got it in her head that she could one day—if she worked hard enough and believed hard enough—be a star? At first, the likelihood of that happening seemed pretty slim: I would just roam around my house belting out *Little Mermaid, Lion King,* and *Beauty and the Beast* songs. A Disney diva! I guess you could say I was a bit of a ham. I was always outgoing—the only comment that my teachers would ever have on my report cards was "Jamie talks too much."

Mom and Dad noticed early on that I liked the spotlight and enrolled me in the dance lessons most little girls take. I started at age three with class twice a week. The steps were not all that intricate: tap your toe, raise your arm, wiggle your butt, and try not to step on the kid standing next to you. At age six, I graduated to The Martha Meredith School of Dance where I studied jazz dance, ballet, tap, and musical theater. The latter consisted of a class in which you'd come in and lip-sync two of your favorite songs. I chose songs by Samantha Fox and Paula Abdul—to a first-grader, they were the epitome of coolness. I was going five times a week now, and slowly becoming more serious about performing. Not that I let it stop me from keeping up with the men in our family: With two brothers, it was kind of a given that I'd be into sports, too. My mom would pick me up from dance class, and, over my tights and tutu, I would put on my cleats and uniform to go to soccer and softball practice.

During my second year in musical theater class, my teacher announced we'd be doing *Annie* for a year-end recital. I was so psyched; I wanted to be Sandy (yes, Sandy is the *dog*). But the teacher saw something in me (I guess it wasn't canine) and cast me as Annie instead. I sang "Dumb Dog" from the movie version of the musical, and while it was far from my finest hour, at least I hit all the right notes. The audience (mostly our families) applauded enthusiastically. I thrived on it, and I decided right then and there that I wanted something else . . . singing lessons. My poor parents.

My mom took me to a studio called Stars of Tomorrow—the name alone convinced me that this was the place for me. The owner, Wendy, gave me a lot of support and helped me a great deal in developing my voice. I did tons of solos in her classes. I even left dance class for a little while to just focus on my singing. After a short time, Wendy said she felt I was ready for professional theater. Did I want to audition? I was eight, and I was like, "Yeah! Yeah! Yeah!" Hey, who wouldn't want to see her name in lights on some Broadway marquee? But my parents weren't too keen on the idea. They thought singing would be a fun little extracurricular activity for me—not a career move, and certainly not when I was still in elementary school. My mom said, "Well, she has school, and I don't want her grades to suffer." But my parents could see how much I wanted it—performing was in my blood—and they knew I would never be happy if I didn't at least give it a try.

Wendy recommended us to an agent, who in turn sent me out for a *Les Misérables* audition. *Les Miz* was one of the biggest shows in the history of Broadway—a huge deal if I got in. The character was the little girl, Cosette. All I knew about her was that she was the face on the poster (no pressure there . . .). So I listened to the soundtrack over and over every day, until I knew her solo, "Castle on a Cloud," by heart. It was a really sweet song about being safe, loved, and in a better place.

I went into the audition feeling pretty good about myself and how I sounded singing the solo. Then I took a look around the room: Oh my God, I was so totally out of my league! There were all these little girls with pictures and portfolios—they were pros and I was pathetic. My mom and I were clueless. We'd never been to an audition before. I didn't know how it worked, I didn't know what to do. The only picture my mom had was my fourth grade school picture that she carried in her wallet, so that's what I walked in with for my audition. Maybe they thought it was cute and refreshing, because they didn't kick me out. They let me sing, and then they told me "Thanks, you can go home now."

I thought that was it. So much for my big Broadway break. But I got a callback . . . and then another. I really was beginning to believe I'd get it, but then it turned out I was too tall. For child actors on Broadway, the shorter the better, because that way you can be in the show longer. Go figure! I remember crying—it was my first time getting rejected and it's really tough not to take it personally, especially when you're eight years old. I remember thinking, "What's wrong with me? Am I not good enough?" And my family was so supportive and tried to reassure me I was special and talented. But you know, sometimes, when you're hurting, it's hard to hear anyone else's voice but your own—especially when your own is shouting, "You blew it!"

Student by Day, Actress by Night

Eventually, I got over it—really because my mom and dad just kept telling me there'd be other parts, other shows. And there were: Wendy told me about a community theater on Long Island that was holding auditions for *The Sound of Music*. It was literally two weeks after my big *Les Miz* letdown . . . and I got the role of Marta, one of the Von Trapp kids. The theater had seats on three sides of the stage. It sat about 250 people and it was very intimate—you could see all the faces in the audience and hear their laughter and reactions. The theater soon became my home away from home.

It was the best first experience for me, because there

were all these kids to share it with, and since I was the second to youngest, everyone especially looked out for me. I remember literally grabbing on to the boy who played Kurt when the captain blew his whistle for our first entrance of the show. My knees were buckling. But, I swear, once I got on stage, it was heaven. The fear melted away. I did the show for eight weekends, all the way through the summer. We even did a stint at a dinner theater, and I learned so much. For example, there are so many mishaps that happen on stage that the audience never sees; as an actor, you get really adept at covering them up. Like the time I broke my toe kicking a bed knob . . . and didn't miss a beat. I was in agony, but the show must go on (even if I had to limp through to the closing curtain).

Performing felt natural to me—kind of like I was just playing pretend with one of my friends. And I could feel the energy in the audience. There's nothing like it and really no way to describe it except "electric." Because that's how it feels—like you're totally charged and you can be or do anything. Every Friday, Saturday, and Sunday I got to feel that way. During the week, I was just a regular kid in school doing my thing, but on the weekends . . . I was an actress, in a dressing room, taking bows. It was pretty wild.

I did one production after another. I continued singing lessons with Wendy but added classes at the theater as well as dance at the American Theater Dance Workshop (which I would do through the end of my senior year in high school). Of course none of my friends understood any of this—they thought it was cool and all, but they just didn't relate to how I felt about performing. It was just, "Oh, Jamie has this weird little hobby. . . ." I was busy, that's for sure, but I don't feel like I really missed out on all that much. Maybe a few sleepovers and some Bar and Bat Mitzvahs, but otherwise, I did all the normal things kids do. As a matter of fact, I think performing gave me quite an education, one that you can't get in school.

From auditioning for professional productions in New York, I learned quickly that it's not always the most talented person or the most hard-working person who gets the part; sometimes, appearance is the deciding vote. Practically every audition, I'd get asked, "Just exactly *how* tall are you?" Ugh! The tall thing again. Before I got to sing or dance or do anything, they wanted to know my height. I was always about two inches too tall (I'm now 5'6") and sometimes that would automatically disqualify me. Was it fair? No, but what can you do about it? I wasn't going to be getting any shorter—just the opposite.

I guess I tried to play it down: I'd wear flat sneakers or kind of slump over, anything to make myself look litt-tle. Of course, it rarely worked and I still got rejected a lot. When I think about it now, maybe being judged that way did impact the way I saw myself later on in life. Maybe the emphasis on the way I looked planted a little seed in my head: "Jamie, you have to look perfect or people won't like you." When people are judging you on what's outside and not inside, it's very hard *not* to feel insecure.

My parents certainly never encouraged me to change anything about myself to get a part—and there were many stage moms who did pressure their kids. There were also lots of moms who refused to take no for an answer—so much for "Don't call us, we'll call you." I was lucky. Mom and I just kind of stood quietly in the corner at these auditions, while the other moms screamed and carried on when their daughters were deemed "Too tall, too short, too skinny, too chubby, too *whatever.*" As if this one part was the most important thing in the world and everything depended on it. Now I can look back and think, "How totally crazy to put so much emphasis on something so insignificant."

Of course, hindsight is 20/20. I'll admit that at times I wished I was different; I wished I was exactly what the director was looking for. But as I got older, I began to believe more and more that everything happens for a reason. You get certain parts and you lose others. Here's my philosophy: Life has a funny little way of working out. You wind up where you're supposed to be—it may not be the path you hoped to take, but you eventually arrive at your destination. I do believe in destiny, or at least I trust that I can't always see the big picture, so what looks like trouble or confusion or just plain *hell* right now can one day turn into the best thing that's ever happened to you. Why? Because everything you do, you should learn from—if not about the world, then at least about yourself. That's how you grow. And you know what? Everyone has to go through growing pains. I went through mine back then and I'm still going through them today. I hope I always am—even if it hurts—because you should never stop growing, never stop challenging yourself, asking yourself tough questions, or reaching for something that's out of your grasp at the moment. I may have been too tall for half the roles on Broadway, but I appreciate it now: When you're tall, you're that much closer to reaching the stars.

2

Love, Loss, and a Dangerous Decision

The Plaza Playhouse in Long Island where I performed for ten years (it's now called The Cultural Playhouse) was, in many ways, just like high school. There were cliques, there was competition . . . and there were crushes.

Brad Stoll was four years older, and I had it *bad* for him. I first noticed him as the cute boy who played Pinocchio at the Playhouse. Later on, we did *Annie* together at the Plainview Y (I was Annie). Then we did *Gypsy,* and I was Baby Louise and he was a newsboy.

He was so sweet and incredibly talented—I followed him around and hung on his every word. I made a complete fool out of myself, but thankfully, Brad didn't seem to notice or hold it against me. We were all friends at the Playhouse, but the two of us had a special connection. He had a manager already, and he was auditioning in New York City all the time for plays, movies, commercials, and TV shows. One day, when I was performing on a telethon with Bob McGrath from *Sesame Street*, he videotaped it and sent it to his manager, Lois. Well, because of that, she signed me, too, and I started going on bigger auditions in the city. I even got a few commercials (one for AT&T) and voice-overs.

My friendship with Brad grew, as did my crush on him. In the summer of 1993, when he was fifteen and I was twelve, Brad was auditioning for the lead in Neil Simon's next movie, *Lost in Yonkers,* along with dozens of other boys. I had seen the play already and thought it would be a great present to take him to see it before he auditioned. So my mom bought us tickets and drove us into the city. She let us see it alone (a major deal—my first date sans supervision!) and then took us to dinner and bought us shirts that said "Almost Famous."

Brad went on numerous callbacks for the role, and on the last one, he wore the shirt. Neil Simon told him, "Well, Brad, you can take off the 'Almost.'" He got it! It was such a great moment for him. From that day on, Brad was my role model, my proof that if you stick to your goals, you'll one day succeed.

And I did. Soon I landed my first "big break" too: the

touring company of a musical version of *It's a Wonderful Life.* How psyched was I? I was cast as a young Mary (Donna Reed played Mary in the 1946 classic movie), and it meant leaving seventh grade for the first half of the year to travel thirty-nine states with the company. My parents were against the idea of me being away from home and school for so long. None of that really worried me—the idea of seeing the country sounded pretty awesome. But my dad was a tough sell. I actually had to argue my case to him, explaining why I wanted to go and how it would benefit me (I would have made a great attorney!). Finally, he gave in and off I went. My mom and my grandma switched off chaperoning me every month and I had a tutor to make sure I kept up with my studies. The only downside was missing my friends and family back home. And of course, I missed Brad. But we wrote each other letters (this was before the days of email or two-way pagers), and before I knew it, I was home again and we were hanging out.

As we got older, we slowly lost touch, but since we shared the same manager, we kept tabs on each other. The year I turned sixteen, I hadn't heard about him in a while. Then I got a phone call: Brad had died. He had been battling Hodgkin's disease and finally his body gave out. He was the same age, twenty-one, that I am right now. It was really hard for me to deal with him being gone. I had never known anyone who died, especially so young. Even now, when I think about it, it knocks the wind out of me.

I still have the picture of us, on the day he got the part in *Lost in Yonkers*. He's wearing the "Almost Famous" shirt and he looks so, so happy. That's how I will always remember him. It's amazing how people come in and out of your life so quickly. But you don't need a lot of time to touch someone and make a difference—that can happen faster than a heartbeat. It did for me, and I know that Brad is watching and rooting me on from wherever he is right now.

My Quest to Be the Best

Don't get me wrong, following your dreams and sticking to your guns is a great thing. I saw through Brad's example as well as my family's that hard work and perseverance do pay off. But somewhere along the way, during junior high and high school, I got a little carried away. I was constantly pushing myself to be the best at everything (school, sports, performing) because I thought if I was any less, I would disappoint everyone—my family, my teachers, my coaches, my friends. I was wrong. No one was telling me I had to live up to these ridiculously high expectations. I was the only one cracking the whip and criticizing myself. It wasn't as if my family was pushing me to be an overachiever. My brothers did their own things, and I never felt like I had to compete with them. My parents weren't demanding I bring home straight A's. It was just my own ambition driving me crazy. I had to be "Perfect Jamie," because that was the image I thought people had of me. But you see, in my own mind, I was anything *but* perfect. In fact, I constantly compared myself to everyone else and agonized, "Are they better than me? Smarter than me? Prettier? More talented?" I reasoned that I could never slow down or just let things slide because that meant people would find out I was a fraud.

With my self-image so fragile, the door was wide open for problems to develop. An eating disorder just sort of snuck up on me, but once it was there, my life was like Alice falling down the white rabbit's hole. I couldn't climb back out, and what was worse, I couldn't even see the light at the top anymore.

It's hard to pinpoint exactly how and when it all started, but I remember once hanging out with a group of girls—there were five of us in a room just chatting and it came up. Someone asked, "Hey, did anyone ever make herself throw up?" Everyone said yes but me. They were like, "Really, Jamie? *Never?* Why not?" I felt dumb—completely clueless. One friend asked if I wanted her to teach me. I was kind of grossed out and said no. But it made me wonder, "Am I wrong because I'm the one *not* doing this? Is everybody doing this?"

It certainly seemed that way, especially when I got to high school. I had a friend who used to throw soda on her lunch so she wouldn't eat any more of it. And there was always talk: "Oh, I'm *sooo* fat! I hate my ass! I feel so huge today! I have *got* to lose weight before the prom!" It scares me to think that so many teenage girls think that purging or starving themselves is not only acceptable behavior but a *cool* thing to do. It's not cool; it's not healthy; it's not smart or sophisticated. And it's not something you need to do because you think it will make you one of the "in crowd." Ironically, all my friends eventually figured that out while I, on the other hand, went on to develop a serious eating disorder.

I think there were several factors that led to my problem. Obviously, I was concerned with how I measured up to my peers—especially when I started going out with my first serious boyfriend in my sophomore year of high school. We went out for seven months (yes, I still remember the exact amount of time . . .) and we were the total PDA couple. It was pretty sickening to be around us. Our friends used to make fun of us, how we could never *not* be holding hands or hugging or making out (not in front of our parents, of course).

My big competition (or at least, that was how I saw it) was his ex-girlfriend. She was thin—*so* thin—and around her, I felt *humongous.* I remember I was lying on the beach with my boyfriend one day, my eyes were closed, and I heard someone mention her name. My stomach sank—there went our lovely afternoon. She walked over and it was like a scene out of a movie: Her hair was blowing in the wind, she had the perfect body, and she practically floated on air. I felt disgusting next to her—a beast! All I could think was "What the hell is he doing with *me?* He is *so* going to get back together with her, I know it."

All these crazy thoughts started running through my head. My boyfriend didn't do anything; it was just me feeling negative about myself. I think a lot of girls do that—they worry how they compare to someone's ex. Well, the more relationships I have gone through, the more I realize an ex is an ex for a reason—even if she does have the body of a supermodel. But it was my first real boyfriend, and I was dealing with all of these new emotions and situations. I lived in constant dread that he was going to dump me. Then guess what? One day, he did.

We broke up over the phone—not even in person! I was at my friend Sloane's house, sleeping over before Halloween so we could get into our costumes for school together the next morning. He called and I could hear that something in his voice was different. Cold, I asked him what was wrong over and over.

Finally he said it: "I don't know why, but I don't want

to be together anymore." I was stunned. It felt like he took a knife and stabbed me in the heart. I tried to keep it together, to not freak in front of him. I didn't want him to have the satisfaction of knowing how much he had hurt me. So I told him I didn't want to talk to him for a while and that I had to go. Then I cried on Sloane's shoulder for what seemed like forever. I called my mom and she picked me up and I cried all night. The next morning, she woke me up and we played Gloria Gaynor's "I Will Survive" on my stereo and danced and sang it about ten times. Then I went in late to school—with sunglasses on. I cried a lot for the next week.

I was devastated—and of course, I thought the reason he broke up with me was I wasn't as pretty or as skinny as his ex or some of the other girls in our school. So it started innocently enough with, "I'll just lose five pounds so the next time he sees me, he'll be like, 'Wow!'" The best revenge is looking great, right? "Hey, guy, look what you're missing!" I didn't understand anything about dieting at the time; I didn't know the difference between a calorie and a fat gram. But the more I read, the more I thought, "Okay, I can do this. No big deal. You just cut back on this, don't eat that, and exercise a lot and you'll look amazing." So I got down to business—my own regime, of course, no healthy eating and exercise plan that I had read about, because I had to do it *my* way. My personal life was completely in chaos, but this—my weight—was something I could control.

I didn't really talk to anyone about my plans to start exercising and eating differently—I just jumped right in. At first, my parents thought it was great that I was showing an interest in being "healthy" but I don't think they knew why I was doing what I was doing—or how I was doing it. I kept a food journal every day. It started out pretty normal, you know, "Breakast: cereal and juice; Lunch: turkey sandwich; Snack: frozen yogurt," and then whatever Mom made us for dinner. But each week, my list of meals got shorter and shorter: "Monday: two egg whites, one stick of gum, two Diet Pepsis." I liked the high I got from seeing that scale go down, down, down. I was good at this. Not only was I accomplishing my goal to lose a few pounds, I could lose even more. Another five. Another ten! Maybe twenty! Not once did it dawn on me that the word "die" is part of the word "diet." If it had, maybe things wouldn't have gone as far as they did.

3

A Slow Form of Suicide

When you're a teenager, the whole world is open to you. There are endless possibilities, so many things you can do, try, see, and experience. As awesome as that all sounds, it's also incredibly scary and overwhelming at times. It's easier than you might think to lose control, lose yourself, and not even be aware of it until it's too late. That's how it was for me with my eating disorder. At first, it was my way of controlling things that were out of my control. Then, it controlled me.

The hardest part of having an eating disorder is you rarely recognize you have one—and you certainly don't want to admit it to anyone—not your parents, not your friends, not your teachers. You just feel that something isn't right inside you. You hate yourself, your life, and eventually, even being around people. You lie, you hide, you keep secrets. Your life is out of control, and the only thing you can control is what you eat—or don't eat—and how much you weigh. Food is the escape route, but there's something underlying that obsession. You hurt yourself and those close to you. You get angry; you get frightened; you feel like no one understands you or notices you. And all the while you're crying for help and no one hears you. They call it a slow form of suicide, and they're right. Having an eating disorder is as abusive on your body as doing drugs or downing alcohol—and it's equally addictive.

Before I go on, let me say this: These are not some lines from a script—all of this is what I felt and what I lived through, although I couldn't see it at the time. I'm not a doctor. I don't know specifically what you need physically or emotionally if some of the above sounds a little too familiar. All I can do is tell you what I did and why I think I did it. I'm very lucky; some girls don't get over it and some girls die. I'll be totally honest with you: I feel like I'm healthy now and I can handle my problem, but it's something I will have to deal with for the rest of my life, like it or not. It stays a part of you—like a scar. You can be healed, but it's still there, even if it's just a faint reminder. I'm glad; I don't want to forget where I was or how bad I felt or how close I came to destroying myself. I carry a photo in my wallet. It's me at my lowest point, weight-wise and emotionally, and every time I look at it, I shudder. I couldn't even fit into a size 0—I was wearing little kids' clothes. I never want to be back there again, and I will fight to make sure I never am. I am also surrounded by great people who make sure I don't let history repeat itself, great people at home and on *The Sopranos* set who love me and care about me. To them, it doesn't matter what I weigh, only that I'm happy and healthy.

Can We Talk?

Girls tell me that it helps to hear someone voicing what's going on in their heads. So I talk about my eating disorder. I talk about it all the time and I'm not ashamed or scared anymore of what people will think or what the tabloids might write. I guess I "came out," so to speak, when I turned eighteen. I did it for a number of reasons: 1. Because I'm young, and I think girls can relate and maybe I can get through to and help some of them, and 2. For myself. I wanted to make something good out of the bad.

I never really thought about going public with my problem. At first, I was embarrassed by it, and I worried how people would react, especially fans of *The Sopranos.* In our first year, I used to go on the show's official Web site and read what the viewers were saying about the cast, the characters, and the show. I loved it. It was so cool to read "Meadow, you go girl!" and be praised for my acting. However, as the second season began to air, some of the fans turned on me. They would post *horrible* things, mostly about how "fat" I got. Yes, I gained weight. My metabolism went wacko from all those months of starvation mode, and as soon as I started to eat normally again, the pounds came back too quickly. I was so determined to show people that I was all better, I had beat this eating disorder, that I was eating *a lot.* I still didn't know how to take care of myself the right way. I kind of expected fans to think I had gotten heavier, but I didn't think they would say anything. Then when they did, it hurt. And you know what? No one would ever say that to a guy.

What no one knew was that Meadow didn't get fat, Meadow got healthy and was able to lead a happy life. Maybe it's not the look that fans wanted to see, but I felt pretty good about the fact that I got through this disorder and I survived. I was a stronger person for it. I think I'm now at a good place—it was about me finding a balance. Unfortunately, I had to find it on TV in front of millions of *Sopranos* fans! And that sucks, plain and simple. I hate when they rerun the old episodes or relcase them on video and DVD. I'm embarrassed especially when I know that people were watching and thinking "Wow, Meadow blew up." I guess—unknowingly—*The Sopranos* helped me chronicle my battle with an eating disorder. There it is, for all to see.

But did I have the courage to announce that to the world? Could I confess that the reason I looked so different from one season to the next was I had a serious problem? Did I need to explain myself or prove something? Why couldn't people just accept me for who I was and not judge me?

I didn't know how to react or what to do, so I cried. A lot. Good thinking, Jamie, that always solves things. And as stupid as it seems, each week I would go back online to see what else they had to say about me ("Is Meadow looking chubby these days or what?"). I was a glutton for punishment. I spent many nights wondering how I could turn this around, how I could just be happy that I got healthy and not allow these cruel comments to derail my recovery. So one morning, I woke up at 5 A.M. and contemplated: "Do I go back to my old ways or do I go on my computer and write a letter to the fans coming clean about what I went through?" I went with the second choice. I wrote a long letter explaining my eating disorder and how hard it was for me to read what people were posting. I begged them to think twice before they lashed out at someone. I'm not just a character, I'm a person with feelings. I told them that those who sought to hurt me did their job, but that I wouldn't let it bring me down. Instead, I was going to come out and help girls who were suffering as I once did.

Then I followed up my words with action. I did my research and contacted EDAP, an eating disorders organization, and said I wanted to get involved. Soon, I was writing articles in *Seventeen* and speaking out at events and fundraisers. I even talked about my problem on *The View* and was profiled as an exercise bulimic in *Rosie* magazine. It was an incredible feeling: freeing, empowering, like a tremendous burden had been lifted. And the reaction was more positive than I ever anticipated: People reached out to me and applauded my honesty. Fans posted apologies on the Web site: "We didn't mean to offend you, we're so sorry. We didn't know." No platinum CD or blockbuster movie could beat the way I feel every time I get a letter from a young girl thanking me and recounting her own story. The letters keep coming, tons of them, every day: "Jamie, you make me feel like I can get through this," "Jamie, you're the only one who understands how I feel," "Jamie, thank you for being so brave."

Skin and Bones

I wish more people would be brave and share their experiences. If I had someone telling me "Hey, you're not alone" maybe, just maybe, I would have confronted my problem—and beat it—before it got out of hand. There arc millions of teenagers suffering. I wasn't some unique case and there was no special reason why this happened to me; I had a great childhood and a loving family and yet this still happened. There is no finger of blame to point at any one thing or person or event. It was several factors all adding up to one outcome: I was starving and exercising myself to death.

Some girls with eating disorders look in a mirror and have delusions that their emaciated bodies are grossly overweight. That wasn't the way it was for me: I knew *exactly* how awful I looked, how skinny, sickly, and pale. I couldn't stand mirrors because it was too painful to see what I'd become—all those bones sticking out. On a hot May day, I had to wear jeans and long sleeves to school because I looked so scary showing any of my body! Yet I became a slave to my eating and exercising routine. I could only eat a certain amount, a certain way, and I had to burn every calorie off . . . or else. Or else what? Or else, I feared, I'd have a breakdown.

I remember saying to my mom, "I'll go crazy if I can't exercise." Because I had so many activities to do in a day—school, clubs, rehearsals—I needed to get up at 4 A.M. to fit in "enough" exercise. If I didn't, I'd spend the whole day miserable, beating myself up that I was a failure, and worse, I became hysterical that I would be fat and ugly. I worked out for at least two and a half hours in our basement before the sun came up; I'd run on the treadmill then do a workout video: "Abs, Buns, Thighs of Steel," "Cardio Blast," and so on. After a while, my parents caught on and begged me to just relax and sleep later. I would hear them calling my name as I went down to the basement to work out. I ignored them. It was easy to tune out everything but my obsession.

For breakfast, I'd eat three scrambled egg whites and two tomatoes. Lunch was a scooped out bagel with mustard or some raw veggies. I'd have a Diet Coke before dance class and a fat-free yogurt for dinner. I eliminated all fat from my diet and I was consuming no more than 400 to 500 calories total a day. Someone as active as I was should have been taking in 2,200 calories a day. I always had to know the *exact* calorie count of everything I ate—even a piece of gum. I threw up a few times, but I hated it. It was so disgusting, and I felt horrible afterwards. Plus, purging destroys your esophagus and vocal chords, and singing was my life. I also flirted with the whole, "chew your food and spit it out" deal: You appear to be eating, but you're never swallowing anything—just hiding your food in a napkin.

My obsession escalated. Everything I did had to be a form of exercise so I could work off any calories I consumed. If I made my bed, I would do knee bends and squats as I tucked in my sheets. As I set the kitchen or dining room table, I'd walk back and forth several times, taking out each fork, knife, plate, or spoon individually. I'd bring my dirty laundry down to the basement one piece at a time, walking up and down the stairs a dozen times or more. And at school, I'd be sitting in class, constantly lifting my leg. When my friends asked why, I said my legs hurt from dancing. The truth was I had read that fidgeting burned calories.

It was hard to hide my strange habits from my family. I remember going to a restaurant with my mom and dad, and I had figured I could allow myself 600 calories for dinner. So I assumed that 300 of those calories would be the bread (I was off, overestimating by about 200 calories). Then the waitress brought it out and the bread had cheese on it. I burst into tears because now I couldn't eat it. My parents were like, "Jamie, what is wrong with you? Just eat it. You exercise so much and you're growing." But it went in one ear and out the other. All I kept thinking is, "They don't understand. They don't know what will happen if I eat that."

Another time, we went to my grandma's house. She's an amazing cook. She had made fried chicken and mashed potatoes and all this great comfort food that I love . . . but I wouldn't let myself eat it. I lied and told her I didn't feel well and I went upstairs to lie down on the bed. My mom came up to see what was wrong and found me sobbing.

I think my mom was the first one who really suspected this was more than just normal teenage angst or rebellion. She would always drive me to my dance class after school and bring me a slice of pizza and a Diet Pepsi. I picked at the pizza; it was really just the Diet Pepsi I allowed myself. Well, one day, she got regular Pepsi instead, and I freaked, absolutely *freaked.* I wouldn't touch it, not a sip. She said, "Jamie, you're being ridiculous, and if you don't stop this business of 'I can't eat this, I can't eat that,' you're going to develop an eating disorder."

Of course, I totally denied it: "What are you talking about? I would *never* develop an eating disorder!" I insisted. And I really believed that. I thought, "No way, not me. I'm much smarter than that." Miss Perfect, you see, would never have a problem. Was I ever wrong. In trying so hard to succeed at everything, I failed at the most important thing of all. Look what I had done to my body. And look what I had done to my life and my family's lives: I threw us all into a nightmare. I was sick, and I had to face that.

In my mind, it wasn't a problem. I was just doing what I should be doing: exercising and eating "healthy." But that wasn't it at all. I was obsessing, and my obsessions were beginning to consume my life. I was crying all the time, and I was so weak and tired, I was falling asleep in class. As a result, my grades started dropping.

Yet, amazingly, I didn't stop—I couldn't stop. I got thinner and thinner, until kids at school were telling me how awful and ugly I looked. I was a skeleton. My eyes were sunken in, my hair was falling out, and I was growing hair in other weird places on my body (a lovely side effect of starvation). I'd catch a glimpse of myself and I didn't recognize the girl who stared back at me. My mom would cry every time she hugged me because she could feel all the bones in my body.

I think my parents blamed themselves, too: Why hadn't they seen this coming? Why hadn't they forced me to eat and stop working out like a maniac? But it wasn't their fault. I kept insisting I was fine, nothing was wrong. And I would hide it well—I stopped eating with my family and friends so they wouldn't see how little I was consuming.

My best friend Sloane was the first to confront me and ask what was wrong. She was great. She was one of the few people in high school that expressed her concern in the right way. Rather than criticizing me, she simply said, "Jamie, I'm worried about you. What can I do to help? *Please* let me help." She still is my closest friend in the world, someone who has seen me through hell and back. I can always count on her to help me stay grounded and keep things in perspective. Sometimes, I think she knows me better than I know myself.

Yet at that point, no one could get through to me—

I simply put up walls and wouldn't let them. Not Sloane, not my parents. I felt like I was stranded in the middle of this desert island with no way off, and no way anyone could reach me. Finally, I reached the breaking point.

My parents and I were on our way into the city to go Rollerblading (any physical activity appealed to me—gotta burn those calories). At this point they knew that something was wrong, but they didn't know the tremendous battle that was going on inside my head. I had planned my whole day, like every other day, on a precise time schedule of eating and exercise. We were supposed to leave at 10 A.M., but we ended up going at 11:30, and I freaked. I couldn't bear to have my schedule go off track. I was shaking in the back of the car and crying, not just because I was frustrated about being late, but because I was terrified that I felt this way. Why couldn't I have just been fine with leaving at 11:30? Why couldn't I look forward to going out to eat with my parents? Why I didn't I ever go to the mall for pizza with my friends anymore? Why couldn't I just be *normal?*

I hated it. I hated myself. I hated my life. Then the words went through my head: "I don't want to live anymore." Oh . . . my . . . God. Did I really want to *die?* I had my whole life ahead of me—yet I was so miserable, I wanted to end it. I had to put a stop to this. I leaned over and cried to my parents: "I have an eating disorder. Please help me!"

My dad pulled the car over and we all cried and hugged. We went straight home and talked for hours. I told them everything that had been going on for the previous seven months. They were shocked and scared. "I can't stop," I admitted. "I don't know how."

The Long Road to Recovery

The next day I was in a psychiatrist's office. I was terrified. I had never been to any kind of therapy before and I didn't know what to do. So my mom came in with me. I remember being embarrassed in the waiting room—like everyone was staring at me and passing judgment: "There's Jamie—the crazy one!" I shouldn't have felt that way. Everyone was there for the same reason, to get help and to get better.

The first session, my mom came in with me and she did most of the talking. I just cried and cried. The therapist was a pretty, soft-spoken woman with a gentle, soothing voice. She gave me a relaxation tape to bring home and told me to listen to it all week until I saw her again. I did, and it was amazing. It was the first time in the longest time that I was able to shut off my brain for a little while. It was the start.

I began to go more often to the therapist, and each

time, I was able to open up more. Therapy helps you take off the blinders and see things as they really are. After several sessions, it started to feel less like seeing a shrink and more like talking to a friend. I actually began to look forward to my therapist visits, because I wanted to tell her how I was progressing and show her that I was getting better. She taught me how to confront what was wrong (the control issue) and also how to approach my friends and family and explain to them what I was dealing with and how they could deal with it, too.

At the same time I was seeing another doctor (I dubbed him "The Medicine Man") who prescribed the ever-popular antidepressant Prozac. The first time I met with him, he weighed me and said, "Now, Jamie, you can either cooperate or go into a hospital. So which will it be?" So rude! That shook me up—and I never really clicked with him because of it. Thank God I had my other doctor to help me keep a positive outlook.

After a few weeks, I was recommended to a nutritionist as well. I thought it was going to be horrible because I didn't want to show someone what I was eating—or how little I was eating. I mean, it was one thing to be admitting and acknowledging the problem, but to fix it was a big step. It ended up being really hard but *wonderful*. At first, I thought about lying and saying I was eating more and exercising less than I actually was, but I realized that the only person I'd be lying to was myself. So it took a while, but the nutritionist slowly helped me out of my old patterns into healthy habits. She even taught me that dessert is okay. For this, I am eternally grateful, because I *love* dessert and really missed it.

You should never have to miss out on the sweet stuff in life.

4

Joining "The Family"

It was great news but the worst timing: I had just confronted my eating disorder when *The Sopranos* was picked up as a new HBO original series. I was expected to start filming the first season episodes in June—little did any of the show's cast, crew, or creative team know what had happened to me since we shot the pilot the previous summer. I had lost thirty pounds in seven months, and looked nothing like the girl they'd originally met as Meadow.

I got the part in July 1997 and we filmed the pilot in August. David Chase, the show's creator, thanked us and said, "Well, it's nice to have met all of you . . ." We didn't know if the pilot would get picked up or even if we'd have a first season. I went back to high school in the Fall, forgot about *The Sopranos,* and started worrying about SATs and getting into college. In October, my boyfriend broke up with me; in November my eating disorder took hold. That was the same month I found out *The Sopranos* was a go. I should have been over the moon, but honestly, I was battling so many personal demons at the time, everything else took a backseat as I struggled to get better. The last thing in the world I needed was the added pressure of shooting a series, but I wasn't about to miss this great opportunity—definitely, the biggest in my career. I just had to get well . . . fast.

The news that HBO was ordering a full season was almost as a big a surprise as my getting the role of Meadow in the first place. Up until then, I didn't have the best luck in landing television shows. When I was sixteen, I decided to go up for a few. Up until that point, I had pretty much focused on the stage, so this was a whole new ballgame. First rule? Watch out for those curve balls. I learned that the hard way. I went on my first TV show audition and was met with overwhelming enthusiasm: "Oh my god, you're perfect!" the casting agent gushed at me, "You're just what we've been looking for." Then what happened? Nada. It was just, "Oh, well, we changed our minds."

At the next audition a few months later, the same

thing happened, and again I lost the part. I came so close to getting these two TV shows (I won't say what they were because they aired and then they went off the air—bygones) only to have the rug pulled out from under me. So I announced to my family, "That's it. I'm going to sleepaway camp this summer. I don't want to deal with this." In other words, I quit.

My parents were very supportive—or maybe they just knew that my antishowbiz mood wouldn't last very long. If I felt like I needed a summer away, that was fine. We booked it: I was going to be a C.I.T. at Camp Pontiac in upstate New York with my friends Jamie, Michael, Russell, Troy, Zach, and a bunch of other kids I knew. But suddenly and tragically, my plans changed: my grandfather—my dad's dad—passed away.

I was very sad and shaken up. I adored my grandpa, Sy Sigler. "Pop," as I used to call him, was the best. He had these fake teeth that he used to take out and make funny faces. He always gave us a dollar when he saw us, and he *loved* chocolate. I think I inherited his sense of humor (maybe the chocolate thing, too). He always knew how to make me laugh. I remember at the funeral, my dad cried while he gave Pop's eulogy. It was the first time I had ever seen him cry and it scared me. I knew how much he was hurting. We all were. We had been lucky enough to say our last "I love you"s the night before, but you always wish you had more time—there are so many things I wish I could have told him and things I wish he had been around to see. But I know he's in a good place. I just hope that they have horse race betting in heaven—Pop would really miss that.

So we were sitting shiva at our house (it's the Jewish mourning—friends and family visit, pay their respects, and bring you lots of cookies and coffee cake) when the phone rang. It was my manager, and she apologized for disturbing us during this painful and difficult time, but she had heard about a really interesting audition that was right up my alley. She said the show was called *The Sopranos*—it sounded like a musical. She didn't know much else about it—not even what TV network it was going to be on or what the show was about. Apparently, they were looking for a "sixteen-year-old, Italian-looking girl." It sounded good to her: I could look Italian—and I could certainly sing soprano!

I was game, and my parents didn't object. They thought it would be a good idea for me to get out of the house a little—it was very depressing there. So I went on the audition with my mom (I even brought some sheet music in my bag in case they wanted me to demonstrate how well I could hit those high notes) and they handed me a script. In the scene, Meadow was fighting with Carmela over wanting to go on a ski trip. I read it once or twice, and stupid me, I still though it could be a musical (a weird musical, but a musical nonetheless). Not once did I have a clue this was a drama about a dysfunctional mob family.

I read the scene for Georgianne Walken, the casting director, and she said, "Pretty good. But can you do it again with attitude?" So I did, this time with Meadow really giving Carmela some lip! Georgianne smiled and said, "Thank you," and off mom and I went to lunch and a little shopping.

I thought that was it; I had given it my best shot, case closed. But when we got home, there was a message on our machine: "Could Jamie please come back tomorrow for a second audition?" My mom was excited, but I refused to get my hopes up. I mean, hello? Hadn't I been down this road twice before with those other TV series? I just assumed this one would end up the same way: "Don't call us . . . we won't call you."

So that's the attitude I went in with the next day when I auditioned for David Chase—kind of, "Yeah, whatever . . ." I had no idea who David was and I was really relaxed. I remember he was just this regular guy, so not intimidating, and he was wearing a T-shirt. He asked me to do the same scene again, two or three times. I did it; he thanked me; off I went back home. Two days later, my manager called to say David wanted to see me again—and this time, it was the final round. The instructions were to report back in a week, and "Please stay out of the sun for a few days, you're too tan for camera." Now, *that* was a first—I'd been too tall, too fat, too thin before, but never too tan! I had a week to get pale, so I avoided the sun and exfoliated liked crazy.

The final call was held in a casting office somewhere on the Upper East Side of Manhattan. There were twenty girls in the room. My heart sank: How could I compete with all these actresses? I remember it was so hot in that room—like 100 degrees and no air. They called us in, one by one. I sat there, sweating, too shy to really talk much to anyone. Then I heard, "Jamie-Lynn Sigler." It took a moment for my brain to register that was *me*. I followed the casting director into another room. They asked me a few questions to break the ice. ("So Jamie, what have you been up to since you first met with us?") Then I auditioned for a whopping ten minutes. Can you imagine? All that tension, all that buildup . . . then ten minutes. That's show business for you.

That night they called to say it was down to two actresses, me and this girl, Christy, and they wanted us to both do a screen test. Mom was jumping for joy, I was ready to rip my hair out. This was agonizing! Let me get it or not get it, but enough of the suspense already! And before they hung up, they warned me again: "You're still too tan, so if you want to look good on film, think pale."

I had exactly one week before the screen test, and I didn't even go near a window. I was like a vampire. Anytime I saw sun, I ran and hid. I was loofahing myself like crazy (it's a wonder I had any skin left), and the day of the audition, I slathered on ivory foundation and powder and wore jeans and long sleeves.

This time, I was told to report to the HBO offices. My screen test was held in a huge room, and I read with John Ventimiglia (he now plays Artie Bucco but at the time, he was acting out the role of Tony with me). After the screen test, I signed an agreement saying the producers had seven business days to call me. Those were the longest seven days of my life. Every time the phone rang, I jumped a mile. I was driving everyone crazy. Luckily, most of my friends were away at camp, so they didn't have to deal with me driving them up the walls, too. Then on the sixth night, the phone rang and something told me, "This is *it.*"

My mom answered and I heard her yell, "Oh, my God!" We were all jumping up and down and screaming in our living room. But after about a half and hour, my mom sat me down and said, "Jamie, now I want you to think about Christy and how she must feel right now. Think of what you would feel like." Then we prayed. We thanked God for giving me this role and we prayed for Christy to be happy and get something, too. And I said a little prayer thanking my grandpa, too—I have a feeling he was in heaven watching what was going on and put in a good word for me.

And how's this for bizarre coincidences? Around the time I was trying out for *The Sopranos,* I also auditioned for a musical called *Parade* at Lincoln Center. It was down to the final round, and it was me and Christy again. I later learned that Christy got the part in the play. I was thrilled for her, and I know God was listening when I prayed that night. It worked out perfectly for both of us, and I believe this was the way it was supposed to be. All of those other parts I had wanted . . . if I had gotten them, I would never have done *The Sopranos.*

Like a Virgin: My First Days on the Set

About three weeks after that elated phone call, we had our first "read-through." Translation: the cast, the director, the producers, and the writers gather around a long table to read through the script together. It's your first time meeting the actors you'll be working with, and you get your first glimpse at the storyline. I was curious and nervous at the same time: what if David Chase had been wrong in picking me? What if I didn't click with the other actors? What if they hated me? What if I was still too tan? I took a deep breath: Jamie, get a grip!

It was held in some random studio space in the city— we didn't have our home at Silvercup Studios in Long Island City yet (we now share the space with *Sex and the*

City). Robert Iler was the first one I met—he was playing my little bro, Anthony Jr. He was twelve years old and already a veteran of TV and movies—he'd been "in the biz," he informed me, since he was discovered at age six. He knew everything, and I was so inexperienced. Thank God he was there. He filled me in and prevented me from making a total fool out of myself (although I did a pretty good job of that anyway).

Two weeks after the read-through, we went up to Jersey and filmed the pilot. I blew out my hair that morning and came with makeup and a bunch of clothes—I had no idea they had wardrobe people and stylists who did it for you. Robert just kept shaking his head: "Jamie, don't you know *anything?*" Negative, I was a total TV virgin. They gave me a 2 X 4 trailer with flowers and I thought it was the coolest thing in the world; I now realize it was no bigger than a cubicle. But it had a bathroom, and before we shot, they sent someone in to do my nails. I felt like a princess. (Okay, maybe a Mafia Princess . . .)

I cheerfully reported to the set—with my new manicure—and was shocked to see a girl standing in my spot. Had I missed my cue? Had they replaced me already? What was going on?

Robert rolled his eyes. "She's your stand-in," he explained. "She stands in for you while they check the camera angles and lighting." I made a mental note of that, but had another panic attack a few hours later. We were moving on to a new scene, and the crew called out, "Check the gate." I looked around—what gate? Where's the gate? Robert explained that the "gate" is really the cameras, and it's just a technical term.

I tried to follow Robert's example and play it cool, to not to let everyone see how excited I was. But it was impossible. I wanted to soak it all in and never forget this wonderful experience. I was running around with my disposable camera all day snapping pictures. They must have all been thinking, "Where did they get this kid—and what is *wrong* with her?"

Right off the bat, James Gandolfini (aka Tony Soprano) treated me like his daughter. My first impression when I saw him? Okay, I was a little scared. Jim looks kind of tough (a plus if you're playing a mob boss) and at first glance, you'd probably think, "Okay, the last thing I'd want to do is make this guy mad." Lucky me, Meadow's mission in life is to piss off her parents!

He walked right over and introduced himself: "Hey, Jamie. I'm your dad." Then he smiled. Jim has this kilo-watt smile and he's so warm. From the start, he was always looking out for me. He'd say, "You know, Jamie, you can ask for things or say you want to stop." I hated to rock the boat in any way—I was nervous to ask questions or make a suggestion about my character. He seemed to have a sixth sense of what I was feeling (maybe it was that perplexed look on my face) and he would put his arm around me and say, "What's up?" Then we'd talk and I'd feel better. He helped me feel more confident and comfortable—like I was one of the family and not some geeky kid who had no idea what she was doing. In the first few episodes, all Meadow did was fight with Tony and Carmela, so we'd be screaming at each other, and after a few takes, it got pretty heated and intense. Then, when the director called "Cut!" Edie and Jim would hug me and apologize for yelling: "We're not mad at you—it's Meadow!"

I really learned so much from the two of them—and not because they ever sat me down and said, "Okay, Jamie, this is how to be an actor . . ." It was more through osmosis: I watched them, and I absorbed how they truly *became* their characters. I don't think either of them has any "method" to their acting—nothing you could teach in a class. They just simply are Tony and Carmela Soprano when the cameras roll. That's what I tried to do as well—I just put myself in Meadow's shoes and let her take me where she wants. If it's a serious scene, I'll take a second or two to "get into it." But most of the time, I'm a troublemaker. I'm the one who's always gabbing and fooling around until the director yells, "Action!" If I dwell on it too much ("What's my motivation? How would my character say this?") then it doesn't feel real.

You just jump right in, and if you're as lucky as I am, you have lots of great costars who'll be there to catch you in case you fall.

When we wrapped the pilot, we all hugged and said good-bye. We really weren't sure we'd ever work together again—welcome to the wonderful world of television programming! But even if this was it, I had made some wonderful friends, and memories to last a lifetime.

My mom and me. It's hard to believe I was once that little.

A Sigler portrait for Adam's bar mitzvah: Adam, Mom, me, Dad, Brian.

Looking like a star in my way-cool shades. With my two bros at Universal Studios in L.A.

At age five, I was already into dance. That's me in the front row with the white bow on my head

Dressed up for my dance recital.

A little slugger at age seven.

At eight years old, singing up a storm at Brian's bar mitzvah.

At age eight on a family vacation to St. Thomas.

At age eleven, I played the role of Annie at Hofstra University.

With my theater troupe and my first crush, Brad (wearing the "Almost Famous" shirt my mom bought him). He was the most amazing guy. I was stunned when he died at age twenty, but I carry him in my heart.

With my gal pals at our prom. From left: Carly, me, Samara, Courtney, Sloane, and Lindsey.

On the day of my prom, the Siglers: From left to right, Adam, Mom, me, Dad, and Brian.

Me and my best friend Sloane at Lover's Cove in Cabos San Lucas.

Grandma, Mom, and me partying at Asia de Cuba in the summer of 2000.

With my beloved grandpa Sy and grandma Teddy. I know "Pop" is watching over me from heaven.

I carry this picture in my wallet to remind me that I *never* want to be this thin again. This is me and my mom, at the height of my eating disorder. It broke her heart. When she hugged me, she could feel my bones.

Another picture I keep of me during my eating disorder to remind me how horribly emaciated I looked.

Performing at the Rockefeller Center tree lighting in 2001.

As Cinderella with my fairy godmother, Eartha Kitt, and my prince charming, Paolo. Eartha is a dynamo—she has more energy than a woman half her age.

Marc Anthony is so hot! I was thrilled to meet him at the tree lighting ceremony.

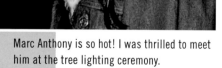

I bumped into Charlotte Church at a charity event. Not only is she super-talented but she's also a sweetie.

With Emme at the Uno party. She's an incredible role model for women and a big inspiration for me.

Ooh-la-la! My friend Nicole (no, not Kidman!) and I do our best *Moulin Rouge* imitation on Halloween 2001.

My manager and best friend A. J. Discala. He's the best!

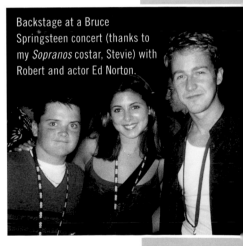

Backstage at a Bruce Springsteen concert (thanks to my *Sopranos* costar, Stevie) with Robert and actor Ed Norton.

When I was in junior high, all the girls wanted to wear Betsey Johnson dresses. Her clothes are the coolest, and she is, too.

Robert and I were psyched to be on *TRL* with Carson Daly. I remember only a year or two before, I had been one of those girls on the street below the studio, screaming for the Backstreet Boys.

Posin' with P. Diddy—the guy rocks.

Me and Justin Timberlake.

I consider Lance a good friend. When we can't get together at events, we 2-way each other. Even with all the fame, he's the most down-to-earth normal guy.

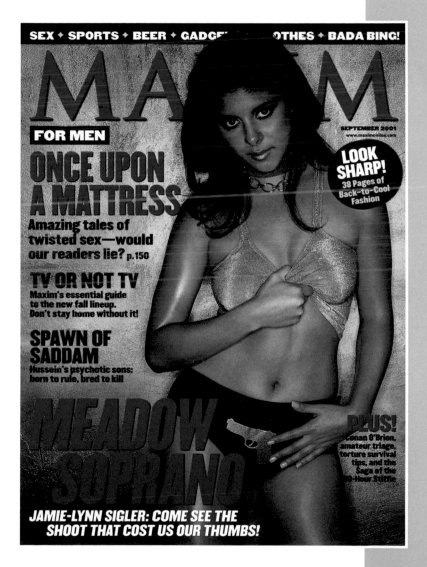

Maxim cover photo

Father knows best: with Jim Gandolfini and Robert Iler during season 3.

He's grown up so much, but Robert will always be my little bro.

With my favorite director, Allen Coulter. He always puts me at ease and encourages me to cut loose when I'm playing Meadow.

At the *Sex and the City* premiere party with my "Uncle Jun." Dominic is such a gentleman.

The fab four, don't you think? Me and Lorraine with her daughters Stella and Margaux at our first Emmy Awards. I did my own hair and makeup, and mom and I bought this dress at Bloomie's.

Ralphie was a rat, but Joe Pantoliano (here, in the hair and makeup trailer with me), is a great guy and a lot of fun.

Looking good on TV takes a lot more work than you might think. Diana, our hairdresser on the set, is a miracle worker.

In season 3, Patrick played my boyfriend Noah. During our sex scene, he was so considerate— he even covered me up between takes because I was paranoid my boobs would show!

At the first season wrap party with *The Sopranos* creator David Chase. I owe him everything. He gave me the greatest opportunity of my life.

Backstage with "my angel" Aida. From the moment we met, we clicked. I wish I had more scenes with Aunt Janice, because we love being together, on-screen and off.

Drea manages to be hip and hot without even trying.

Jason (Jackie Jr.) and I caused quite a stir: everyone believed we were a real-life couple. The truth? Although he's a hottie, we're just friends.

Backstage during season 3 with my "mom," Edie. Off camera, she's much more of a natural woman than Carmela. No big hair or long nails.

Going glam with Kathrine and Drea on the red carpet for the SAG Awards.

All in the family: Me, Edie, Jim, Robert, and Tony at a dinner party.

5

The Skinny on the Set

The last time we had all been together on *The Sopranos* was August. It was now June of the following year, and we were shooting the first full season. I showed up at Silvercup Studios and braced myself for the reaction. I knew how different I looked—even I barely recognized me.

"Jamie, is that you?" asked Jim Gandolfini, trying to make light of it, although I could see the worry on his face. Most people just did double takes but didn't comment. Robert Iler, maybe because he was so young, was pretty upfront with his opinion: "Wow, what *happened* to you?" I just smiled and shrugged. "Uh, nothing." Robert probably didn't know what an eating disorder looked like, but he didn't buy my lame answer. "Yeah, right."

I walked around eating candy to prove to everyone that I was perfectly fine: "Hey, look at me! I love to pig out, see?" I actually made myself sick a few times stuffing my face just to prove this point. The wardrobe people were totally puzzled. I told them I was two sizes bigger than I was (who was I kidding?). They knew I was lying, but were nice enough not to make a big deal out of it. They just layered my shirts to make me look less scrawny.

David Chase knew there was a lot more going on than I was revealing. He called my mom in and asked if I was okay. She played dumb and assured him I was. We left it at that, and I started shooting the first couple of episodes. I was working with my doctors and had gained five pounds back already. I thought everything was fine and that no one on the show was concerned at all. Then one day, a girl in my theater group came up to me, grinning. "I guess you're not going to be on *The Sopranos* much longer," she said. "I just auditioned for your part."

What? My head was spinning. They were actually holding auditions behind my back? I was so angry—not at David, but at myself. I had finally gotten my big break on a TV series, and now, because I had been so stupid, I was going to lose everything. How could I blame them for being concerned that I wouldn't be able to do my job? For worrying that the stress of a weekly TV series could make me even sicker? I think my parents worried; maybe I did a little, too. But I wanted *The Sopranos* so badly that I was determined to recover. An eating disorder is not something you just catch like a cold and it goes away. You have to work at it to get better, both physically and mentally.

Luckily, eating was not an issue on *The Sopranos* set. There is always tons of food around—everything you can possibly imagine. And in case I was too busy to grab breakfast, lunch, or a snack at the buffet, they'd send trays of food to my dressing room. I ate and, eventually, I got healthy; they never had to replace me.

The set is probably the only place I don't overanalyze how many calories I'm consuming. I just dig in when I'm hungry. But let's face it: Diet is always a favorite topic among women. It must be some female gene that men are missing. Do you ever hear guys stressing over cellulite? Or asking each other "Do these pants make my butt look big?" But women can't resist talking and thinking about it. For example, Drea de Matteo and I love to gab about exercise. She is in phenomenal shape, so she gives me healthy pointers. Her rule? You should work out so you can eat *whatever* you want (and she does).

Edie and I always compare stories about how people tell us we're much thinner and better looking in person than on TV. It's like, "Excuse me? Are you telling me I look *bad* on TV? Thanks a lot!" I think every woman on the set understands what I went through to some extent, and around them, I feel incredibly supported and accepted for who I am.

Aida Turturro (she plays my aunt Janice Soprano, Tony's sister) is the person I confide in the most. She's become the big sister I never had. We clicked from the second she stepped on the set, and I can tell her *anything*. We go to lunch and the gym; we get our nails done together; we hang out on the weekends and just girl-talk and vent. She is such an inspiration to me—she loves her body (she's full-figured and proud of it). She's like an angel. Her strength, her confidence, and her joy for life blow me away. And she can always, *always* make me crack up—on the set, in yoga class (we were like Laverne and Shirley in the back of the room, giggling and twisting ourselves into pretzels), in the middle of a photo shoot. I call her "The Hurricane" because she is truly a force of nature. She walks into a room and people are just drawn to her like a magnet because she gives off this beam of positive energy. Whenever I start to doubt or question myself, she's the voice of reason, putting things into perspective for me. She tells it to me straight—no holding back because that's not her style. Aida is my hero.

My *Sopranos* Co-stars

This is my "family." I love them all dearly. You probably think I'm just saying that, but I swear it's true—we love each other and treat each other with the ultimate respect and loyalty. Maybe it's because we're all together at Silvercup and not in Hollywood—we're kind of removed from the rest of the world. There are no egos, no attitude, just people who genuinely care about each other and support each other. From talking to other actors, I know what a rare situation this is, so I have to embarrass my gang, just a little, by sharing how lucky I feel to have them in my life (and now in my book!):

- **James Gandolfini (Tony):**
  I consider him Dad #2. Unlike Tony, who can be hot-headed, temperamental, and irrational, Jim is mellow and laid-back. He's warm and caring —like a big teddy bear—and he looks out for everyone. He's someone I admire on many levels. I also think he's incredibly cool and wonderful to have heart-to-hearts with.

- **Edie Falco (Carmela):**
  She is the most unaffected person I know and a real role model to me when it comes to handling success. Carmela is all about appearances. Edie? She's not at all "high maintenance." Off screen, she'll wear very little makeup, and she hates big hair and long nails. I think of her more as a really cool aunt rather than a mom—someone you are close to but don't feel intimidated by. She is also my favorite actress out there.

- **Robert Iler (Anthony, Jr.):**
  My little bro onscreen and off. I love him to death, and we'll

always have that brother-sister bond (although he is more a man now than a little boy!). He also has the best sense of humor—a real joker! I know on the show he seems kind of dry and deadpan, but in real life he's a riot—and much, much smarter than A.J.

- **Aida Turturro (Janice):**
Unlike Janice who is flaky and flighty (not to mention, quick on the trigger), Aida has her head on straight and is the sanest, most stable person I know. She is my best friend. Any time I need a pick-me-up, she's there with a pep talk to help me put things in their proper perspective. Her energy is contagious. I feel so lucky to have her in my life.

- **Drea de Matteo (Adriana):**
So sweet and such a hip chick without even trying to be. She's got a great sense of style that's all her own—she'd rather start a trend than be a slave to one. She owns this store Filthmart down in the East Village that sells the coolest vintage clothes.

- **Lorraine Bracco (Dr. Melfi):**
She has the best laugh I have ever heard, and she laughs a lot. Dr. Melfi may be reserved and repressed, but Lorraine is boisterous and she throws great parties. It's hard to picture her character letting loose, but trust me, Lorraine knows how to have fun.

- **Tony Sirico (Paulie Walnuts):**
My protector. He has a heart of gold and always wants to know what's wrong so he can fix it. Paulie is dense, but Tony is as sharp as a tack. A little known fact: He does his own hair like that. And he wears this great cologne. I have no idea what it is, but you can always smell him coming.

- **Steven Van Zandt (Silvio Dante):**
Stevie is a rock star, a great actor, and my neighbor—we live

around the corner from each other in Manhattan. He doesn't dress, act or talk anything like Silvio, which makes you realize what an amazing actor he is because you so believe he's this tough-talking mob guy. His wife actually plays his wife on the show, which I think is very cute.

- **Michael Imperioli (Christopher):**
  Don't be fooled by the fact that Christopher has a habit of not using his head. Mike is super-intelligent. He is not only a gifted actor, but a great writer as well. It's a whole other career for him. He writes Sopranos episodes, including "From Where to Eternity," in the second season, which was brilliant.

- **Dominic Chianese (Uncle Junior):**
  The most soft-spoken gentleman I have ever met. He sings opera so beautifully and he's been on Broadway (I am in awe). Uncle Jun has lots of opinions—which he will give you whether you want them or not—but Dominic has a quiet wisdom. I love it when he shares his stories (he has some great ones about working on The Godfather) and when you can hear him humming on the set.

- **Jason Cerbone (Jackie Aprile, Jr.):**
  So not the bad boy. Behind the looks (he used to model), he has a wonderful, warm, funny personality, and we always had a blast working together. What you may not know (but might have suspected from those muscles), he used to compete at bodybuilding.

- **Nancy Marchand (Livia):**
  I miss my "grandma." She was such an amazing actor and such an important part of The Sopranos, the matriarch of the Family. Livia never smiled but Nancy always did. I know in the end it was hard for her because she was so ill, but she never let on. She inspired us all with her strength and her courage, and she lives in our hearts.

How the Cast Came to My Rescue

Some girls bite their nails; some twirl their hair. My annoying little habit? I take on way too much because I think I can handle it. It always winds up a disaster with me trying to cover my butt—or worse, feeling guilty big-time for not fulfilling my obligations. You'd think I would have learned something from my overachieving high school days. Like, maybe I shouldn't spread myself so thin? But, no: Jamie tries to be Supergirl. I'm working really hard on that these days—"No" is a not a dirty word, and I can turn stuff down (events, appearances, interviews) if I have too much on my plate. My manager and boyfriend, A.J., is great at helping me realize this—not only does he tell me never to feel guilty for putting myself and my health first, but if I'm a wimp and don't know how to beg off of doing something, he'll pick up the phone and do it.

I was really guilty of biting off more than I could chew during my second season on *The Sopranos*. I assured everyone involved on the show that I could juggle both the show and taking some college courses at NYU—*no problema!* I discovered pretty quickly it was a *huge problema:* I was having a rough time trying to balance classes, being in a new dorm with new people, and filming. I could feel my stress level rising, but I kept insisting I could do it all (you know how you tell a fib so many times you start to believe it yourself?). I reached the breaking point the day of my first midterm exam The test was at 7 A.M. and I had to report to the set at 10 A.M. To make things even more complicated, we had a cast photo shoot happening at 2 P.M. It should have been fine—I had plenty of time between the test and my filming. Well, it turns out my alarm clock was on my roommate's side of the room and I never heard it go off. The phone rang at 11 A.M., and it was the set, asking "Jamie, where are you?" I, of course, was still in bed, fast asleep. I freaked. I had missed everything. I ran out of the dorm in my pajamas with only my wallet and cell phone and headed for the subway, desperately trying to figure out how I could fix this. On the train, I called my prof and made up some ridiculous story about why I had missed the test (luckily, I got his answering machine and not him).

When I got to the set, frazzled and out of breath, everyone asked me how my exam went. "Oh, fine . . ." I lied. I dashed into wardrobe, hair and makeup, filmed half my scene, then rushed into the studio where everyone was posed and ready to take the picture (they'd all been waiting for me to show up). Finally, I got into place just as the photographer shouted, "Say cheese!" With that, I burst into tears. I just put my head down on Tony Sirico's shoulder and bawled. I couldn't hold it in anymore—all the pressure, all the obligations. I felt like the walls were closing in. I was a mess. I said I could handle everything at once, but I couldn't. In fact, I couldn't handle anything!

Jim came over and put his arm around me. "Everyone put it on hold for a few minutes," he announced, and took me aside. Then he ordered me an eggplant parmesan sandwich and the rest of my castmates gathered around and comforted me. After a few minutes of *Sopranos*-style TLC (hugs, sympathy, and Italian food), I calmed down, and I was able to smile for the camera. My mom picked me up later that day and we talked about what had happened. I decided it was time I stopped trying to be Supergirl. I took a leave of absence from school. I'm happy with my decision, although occasionally, when I visit my friends on their campuses or walk around the Village down near NYU I think, "Did I make a mistake? Am I missing out on this whole great college experience?" I'll go back one day, when I'm ready. My parents were cool with this; they want what's best for me, and right now, that's my health and my sanity.

If there's one thing I've learned over these past few years, it's to appreciate the moment you're in and not rush it away. Life is not some "To Do" list you have to keep checking off ("Education? Check! Career? Check! Nervous breakdown? *Check!*") If you're stressed to excess, you open yourself up to all sorts of problems—in my case, I could have easily relapsed into my eating disorder (thankfully, I didn't). While I was going to college and doing the show, I wasn't doing a good job of either. I was always making excuses, even telling lies, to make everyone think I had it all together. Why couldn't I admit I didn't? Why couldn't I ask for help if I needed it? Why couldn't I take a time-out if I felt overwhelmed, over-tired, or overextended?

When I look back at those few months, they're pretty much a blur. And it shouldn't be that way: That's not living. I was on autopilot, just getting through the day so I could do it all over again tomorrow. Eventually I reached a point where I had to say, "Enough!" I realized life is not about quantity (How much did I squeeze into my schedule today?) but quality (Did I learn something? Did I love what I did?). I think after 9/11, I feel this way even more. So after all I went through, and thanks to my "family," I came away with an important life lesson (something they couldn't teach me in my college classes): Sometimes you should just kick back and appreciate the little things . . . like eggplant parm and great friends to share it with.

Backstage at Silvercup

Each episode of *The Sopranos* (we shoot thirteen a season) involves different characters interacting. So maybe one week I'd have a lot of scenes with Edie and Jim; the following week, Jason Cerbone and I could be paired for practically the whole time. The only time everyone is together is at read-throughs. And that's fun. It's like catch-up time, lots of hugs and hellos and "What's new?" We do sometimes see each other when we're not working—we go see each other's movies and plays, and we're all very supportive of our extracurricular activities.

Everyone was really psyched when I sang in *Cinderella* (they all came to Madison Square Garden to see me in it) and when my CD came out. I used to sing at our *Sopranos* season premiere parties (two years ago I performed "Someone to Watch Over Me" and got a standing ovation from the cast and crew). So maybe the rest of the world is shocked that Meadow has a voice, but not my fellow Sopranos. Dominic Chianese and Stevie Van Zandt sing and both have albums (I saw Steve perform with the Boss and the E Street Band at the Meadowlands—awesome!). I went to see Edie's play *Sideman* on Broadway and Jim's movies—*The Mexican* with Brad Pitt and Julia Roberts and *The Last Castle* with Robert Redford. We've all got a lot going on and that's great. It makes us not only better actors but better people.

But no matter what I have going on, my *Sopranos* schedule is what I work around. We shoot seven to eight months out of the year, most of the time at Silvercup because the soundstage houses our sets. Everything from Meadow's dorm room and the interiors of the Soprano house to the Bada Bing back room, Dr. Melfi's office, and Nuovo Vesuvio (Artie Bucco's restaurant) are on the stages. The rest of the time, we might go on location—usually to Jersey, because that's where Tony runs the business and where he lives (North Caldwell, to be specific). Occasionally, I have a light week with few scenes and I can travel or record or just visit my girl-friends away at college for a few days. This season, I even had a few episodes off—so I got to go to L.A. and shoot a movie *(eXtreme Dating)*.

A typical *Sopranos* day for me might start in the morning between 5 and 7 A.M., but as the week goes on, the call times get later. By Friday, I might not need to be on set until noon—which means I get to sleep in. Yay! I usually have to work three to four days out of the week, depending on how much of a part Meadow plays in the episode's plotline. I'll get to the set (a car picks me up from my Manhattan apartment and takes me out to Silvercup), eat some breakfast, go get hair and makeup done, rehearse. Then usually I have an hour before we shoot the scene. What a lot of people do not know about filming a series or a movie is that you do have quite a bit of downtime: twenty minutes here, twenty minutes there, while they're changing scenery or lights or discussing direction. So I use the time to chat on the phone or my two-way with friends, read some scripts, answer fan mail, even write this book. I also catch up on my sleep—I'm a big napper, so you'll often find me snoozing in my dressing room. I work an average of eight to ten hours a day, and I need the time to recharge my batteries.

Lights, Camera, *Sex!*

For anyone who has ever watched a hot and heavy love scene on screen and thought, "Now that looks like fun," I think you should reconsider. It's not sexy; it's not a thrill; it's not even remotely romantic. And as an actress, it's probably my least favorite thing to do, even when the guy is unbelievably cute and sweet, like Jason Cerbone, aka Jackie, Jr.

The first time Jason and I had to kiss was weird because we were good friends and we used to hang out all the time. So here we are, preparing for a major make-out in an episode. The scene took place in the dorm—Jackie, Jr. takes Meadow home from a frat party because she's really out of it. Jason looked at me; I looked at him. We cracked up. I said, "No offense, Jase, but this feels like kissing your brother." After rehearsal, the director told us to calm down and think about our motivation: "You guys are supposed to be really into each other. You're in love; you're both on Ecstasy. There has to be more wild, uninhibited passion."

"Okay," we decided, "we're both professionals. We can do this." So Jason and I plotted it out—it was very mechanical. "Jamie, do you mind if I touch you here?" "Okay, can I grab you there?" "Finally, after about an hour of choreographing every grope and moan, we gave up and just went for it. It turned out pretty well and looked realistic, considering the fact that the crew was hovering over our heads the whole time ("Smile! You're on *Candid Camera*!"). I guess if you're an actor, you eventually get used to it and it gets easier (if they ever decided to resurrect Jackie, Jr., I think Jason and I could do a better job this time around . . .). Although Edie told me she was very nervous when she had to do a sex scene with Jim for the season two finale, "Funhouse" (in the sable coat Tony brings home for her, remember?). I could tell she had cold feet. She was smoking one ciga-rette after another and pacing around the set.

I had my turn in season three. My sex scene was hard. *Very* hard. At first, I was really concerned about the nudity. I wasn't ready to bare it all! Actually, I wasn't ready to bare *anything* (unless you count a shoulder, an elbow, a kneecap . . .). I'm not sure I'll ever feel okay with showing some extra skin on camera. I guess it would depend on the role. But the director of the episode, Allen Coulter, was really cool and he said he'd work around it. "You won't see anything," he assured me. "It'll just be the *illusion* of being naked."

Uh-huh. Everything sounded good up until the word "naked." All week long, while I was learning my lines, I was dreading having to do it. I mean, I understood it was a big moment for Meadow, a huge storyline for my character and I should have been really excited. I was, but, *hello?* The whole world would be watching—not to mention my mom, dad, grandma, and all my friends who tune in faithfully every week. I felt sick. It wasn't even about me feeling self-conscious about my weight or anything—I was just paranoid my boobs would show.

On the day of the shoot, I tried to be a professional about it: "It's just acting," I reasoned. "It's not like I'm *really* having sex on TV. I can do this. No biggie." I walked into my dressing room and there was a whole array of cones, fringes, and G-strings laid out for me. I nearly had a heart attack: "Oh my god, am I supposed to wear *this?*" Everyone cracked up. Duh, it was a joke. It was the whole Bada Bing stripper wardrobe. But what I wound up wearing wasn't much more concealing. I put on pasties, these little flesh-colored sticky patches that cover your breasts . . . sort of.

Patrick Tully, who played Noah Tannenbaum (my half-Black/half-Jewish boyfriend), was really great. He covered me up between takes so all you could see was my back. And I'll let you in on a little secret: I was wearing sweatpants the whole time under the covers. Lucky for me, Meadow was supposed to be nervous about losing her virginity. So if I looked like a basket case, it actually worked well for the scene.

Aside from the stress of actually shooting the scene, I was totally okay with the idea of Meadow losing her virginity—even if some people objected and thought she was too young. She wasn't acting like a slut; she really had feelings for this guy. She tells Carmela "He's a sensitive and brilliant person" and she truly believes that. At first Meadow was probably attracted to Noah because she knew Tony didn't approve—it was a rebellion thing. You don't like my boyfriend? You're going to act like a bigot? You're going to try to tell me who I can and can't see? Well, take this, Tony! But then I think she fell in love for the first time. The scene was tastefully done and very realistic. Meadow and Noah used a condom, and that was responsible. We didn't put out any kind of message that said, "Hey, teenagers should have sex." It was just my character maturing, feeling and experiencing new things. Was it the right thing for her to do? Well, Meadow eventually learned that Noah was not the man of her dreams (to say the least—he dumps her). But at the time, it was something she was ready for, emotionally and physically.

Meadow has come a long way, and she has a long way to go. You know the rumor about how she got her name? Supposedly she was conceived in the parking lot at the Meadowlands! She started out as a little girl who was just there to drive her dad crazy. But she's now a major influence on her family; they want her to succeed and do everything right because they do things wrong. But you'll see even more in the upcoming episodes that she's finding it hard to live up to their expectations. Meadow is depressed. She's got problems for the first time; she's in therapy, she's taking pills. Tony said it in the second season: "Everyone thinks you're like your mom but you're more like me." And it's true, she's her father's daughter. I wouldn't be surprised if one day, she was running the Family. She's smart; she's knows what's up—Dad is not into waste management, he wastes people. At first, all she wanted to do was run away from it, as far away as should get, which is why she was considering Berkeley. But now, I think she's accepted it. Anthony, Jr., doesn't seem to have it in him to follow in Tony's footsteps. I think Meadow does—she's a lot like her grandma Livia, too. Tough, smart, no-nonsense. She calls it like she sees it, you know?

I've had a lot of favorite moments on the show, many of them with Jim. I love the "College" episode in the first season where Tony takes Meadow to visit Maine to scout out universities. That was the beginning of them really bonding and understanding each other. Jim and I also connected and grew closer. We spent a whole week working together, and we were the focus of the entire episode. I love the scene where Meadow is tipsy and

Tony puts her to sleep in the motel room. He also kind of admits to her for the first time what he really does (she's known all along). We were sorry when it wrapped because it was so much fun being a team, just us two.

And then there's this moment in the kitchen in the episode "Bust Out" from the second season: Tony's drinking and Meadow comes home. You can see it in her face—she wants to say, "I love you, Dad." She wants to cry, she wants to laugh, but she can't. She has to put up this wall or she loses control. Tony's a lot like that, too. The only one he can talk to openly and honestly is his therapist. He's gotta be the tough guy. He sees himself in Meadow and she sees herself in him—and that scares them both.

People are always asking me, "What do you wish your character would do?" Well, maybe the show's writers should take this down: I would love Meadow to go to lunch with her dad, or take her brother out, or go shopping with her mom. I'd like her to do some of the things I enjoy doing with my real family. I would love for her to let down her guard and really bond with them. If I could sit Meadow down, that's what I'd tell her: Love your family for who they are, the good and the bad, because you're a part of them and they're a part of you.

6

Living Large

Y ou need to understand one thing: None of us on *The Sopranos* ever thought the show would take off so quickly and become this big. Not in a million years. We loved it; it was our baby and we were rooting for it. I know Tony likes to say, "Hey, we're just like any other family," but we're so *not*. *The Sopranos* was really bold and different for a weekly TV series (violence, cursing, a mob boss who has anxiety attacks and sees a shrink). To be honest, we had our doubts that people would even get it, much less like it. Did they ever.

I was probably the most floored by all the attention

and accolades (Robert came a close second). It felt like I was walking around in a movie dream sequence: Here I am at the Emmys, here I am on the cover of *Rolling Stone,* here I am on the red carpet being interviewed by Joan Rivers. Someone pinch me 'cause this couldn't be happening! But it was, and the amazing thing? It started before our show even aired.

As soon as the critics got a sneak peek at the pilot, the positive reviews started pouring in. *The New York Times* called us "the best television drama ever made." But it didn't feel real to me until one day I saw the promo on HBO for our "groundbreaking new series." We were getting calls to be on the cover of *TV Guide;* all the women on the show got to be in *Vogue* together. It happened so fast, and it was great because it happened to us all at the same time.

My Scrapbook

Here's what critics were saying about us. I was beyond psyched to see us mentioned in *People*, *Time*, you name it. The reviews were phenomenal:

"The Sopranos hits all the notes . . . it has intelligence and feeling and brutality."   —*People* magazine, 1/18/99
(They also described me as the "teenage daughter growing increasingly alienated.")

"An ironic masterpiece . . . a fresh and unusually realistic yarn."
                    —*TV Guide*, 1/16/99

"Alternately affecting and hilarious . . . [Tony] is an apt '90s antihero: a *paisano* on Prozac."   —*Newsweek*, 1/18/99

"The first wonderful surprise of the 1999 TV season is here, and it's *The Sopranos.* . . ."   —*Entertainment Weekly*, 1/15/99

"The innocence and ignorance of son Anthony pasted against oh-so-knowing daughter Meadow, who's trying to grow up as soon as possible, enhances this definition of insularity of a mob household. . . ."   —*Variety*, 1/4/99

"The Sopranos is distinctive, absorbing, and fresh. . . . Tony's wife, Carmela, can't seem to get along with a teenage daughter named Meadow. Yes, Meadow. . . ."   —*The Washington Post*, 1/9/99

"The Sopranos takes off with the speed of an inside joke. . . . Tony's rebellious teenage daughter is named Meadow (Jamie-Lynn Sigler), a choice perfect in its gauche, wrongheaded attempt to blend into respectable society. . . ."   —*The New York Times*, 1/8/99

"The first gotta-watch, gotta-love, Gotti-like TV series of 1999. . . . It doesn't just hit a high C. Across the board, it's an A-plus."
                    —*The New York Daily News*, 1/8/99

The first time we went to the Emmy Awards, Robert and I were maniacs. We took pictures on the plane—it was the first time either of us had been in first class and we thought it was the coolest thing in the world. "Oh my God, we have our own DVD players!" "Oh my God, we get to make our own sundaes!" We were *insane.* We took pictures in the limo ride en route to the Peninsula Hotel; then we took pictures in our rooms because we couldn't believe how huge they were. The hotel was so glam. Everywhere we went there was another celebrity. We were sitting in the pool with Michael J. Fox (who will eternally be Alex P. Keaton from *Family Ties* to me) and his wife Tracy Pollan. Sarah Jessica Parker walked by and waved (even off screen, she is so *Sex and the City*-chic).

That night we all went to our executive producer Brad Grey's house. It wasn't like a cliché Hollywood party, it was in his home, and it was really relaxed and low-key—just our *Sopranos* gang. We played bocci ball and tennis; we had a buffet; everyone was in jeans and sneakers. We were having such a blast, we didn't even care if we won an Emmy. Although, I have to admit, my fingers were crossed.

The next day was the Big Day. Red carpet, limos, paparazzi . . . the whole nine yards. I didn't know it at the time, but getting ready for the ceremony is just as big a deal as the actual event. Forget a stylist picking out my wardrobe for the evening: Mom and I just went shopping back home and bought a maroon strapless gown at Bloomingdales. I even did my own hair and makeup. The only thing I got help with was my jewelry, because one of the girls who worked on *The Sopranos* had connections. So I borrowed some earrings and a necklace and I was a nervous wreck all night that I was going to lose them. Thanks but no thanks. I think in the future, I'll just wear my own stuff or fake jewels till I can afford the real thing. Knowing you have $200,000 around your neck is way too much stress for me.

If you thought we were bad the day before, you should have seen me and Robert running around that red carpet with a disposable camera ("Holy, shit!" we squealed in unison. "There's Jennifer Aniston and Brad Pitt!") Inside, the whole *Sopranos* cast sat together, and when David Chase won the first Emmy for the show (with James Manos, Jr., for best writing on my favorite episode, "College") we all passed it around and got to hold it. Then Edie won for Best Actress and we also got Emmys for editing and casting. Maybe no one recognized us coming in, but they sure knew who we were coming out.

At the first after-party at Spago's (could anywhere be more Hollywood?) Robert and I were busy searching the room for the cast of *Friends.* The only person we actually had the nerve to go up to was Sarah Michelle Gellar, Buffy the Vampire Slayer herself, and she was so nice. Totally normal and friendly. The second party was HBO's, and we thought it would be low-key like Brad's. We expected just some of the cast and crew of *Sex and the City* and *Oz* to show up, but it turned out to be the hottest and the biggest party in town. And everyone was there . . . to meet us. I, however, was eager to meet up with the *Sex and the City* girls. I practically stalk them. I sneak on their set at Silvercup sometimes to see what they're doing and, more important, what they're wearing. They're always like, "Oh, look, it's Meadow again." It's totally embarrassing to get discovered lurking around Carrie's apartment or ogling Aidan, but I can't help it. I'm a groupie.

I've had several more of these "pinch me" moments over the years. Robert and I were both nominated for *The Hollywood Reporter* Young Star Awards and we won two years in a row. In the past when we went to these things, we always felt like such outcasts. We were from New York, and all the other kids knew each other from L.A. and from working on the same lots. We didn't know anybody. We were up against such amazing young actors (all under eighteen). I didn't expect to win; I never even wrote an acceptance speech the first time, so I was totally unprepared and just blabbered. I also was trying hard not to cry and shake at the podium. I have no idea *why* I was nervous: This was a teen awards show at Nickelodeon studios in California, not the Oscars. But it meant so much to me. I felt like I'd arrived. I was also nominated twice for the American Latino Media Arts Awards (ALMA) which is very cool, because I'm so proud of my Latin roots.

As an ensemble, we've won the Screen Actors Guild Award for Outstanding Performance in a Drama Series. And if there's any doubt of what a close-knit group we are, this should convince you. In 2000, during our first Golden Globe Awards, there was only room for the individual nominees in the ballroom (Lorraine, Edie, and Jim), so the rest of the cast was told to stay downstairs in the party room watching on monitors. Well, Tony Sirico was having no part of that. He grabbed my hand and Robert's and announced, "That award is for all of us, and we should all be there to accept it. Everybody follow me." Picture this: a stampede of Sopranos running through the kitchen and backrooms of the Beverly Hills Hilton in our gowns and tuxes. We hid in the back of the ballroom, and when they announced *"The Sopranos* for Best Series" we stormed the stage. We got in trouble—all these Golden Globe production guys were yelling at us—but it was awesome. We wanted to share the joy and the excitement—Tony knew how much it meant to all of us. Besides, don't those award show people know better? No one messes with the Sopranos.

News Flash: My Love Life

Some people have scrapbooks . . . my mother has our entire house. All the magazines I've been in, the reviews, the editorials—right up there on the walls for all to see. It is so totally embarrassing (the baby pictures were bad enough), but it does make me stop and think: All this is just three years. I grew up reading *Seventeen,* and now I'm in it. I always loved looking through the photos of stars in *InStyle,* and there I am. Interviewers often ask me, "Has it gone to your head—all the attention?" Honestly, I try very hard not to get caught up in the hype. My family keeps me grounded—especially my two brothers, who will always remind me that even though I'm on *The Tonight Show,* I'm still their little sis. And I know how fickle the business can be—who's to say I'll be this lucky forever? Maybe in ten years, people will be saying, "Jamie, who?" I understand that. It's happened to a lot of other actors who wind up in "Where Are They Now?" articles. All I can do is just be grateful and gracious and use the attention I've been given for positive things, not just self-promotion.

Not for one minute do I take for granted how lucky I am. I mean, I've gotten to meet some of the most incredible people, even become friends with them. It's weird: You're at a club and there's some other actor there, and because you're both "famous," people just assume you're together. But sometimes, it does happen that way. You travel in the same circles and, after a while, you become friendly. That's how it was with Lance Bass from 'NSYNC (uh-oh, I can already hear those gossip columnists gabbing . . .). We used to go to the same club all the time in Manhattan, and we ended up talking one night. Now we're good friends (you heard me, just *friends)* and we hang out and talk on two-way. We saw each other at a lot of MTV events and stuff and we spent New Year's together. He's just this great guy who's smart and really fun to be with.

Of course, the media has to make a bigger deal out of stuff than it actually is. Take those Jeter rumors. That got out of control, and it became a little embarrassing. Derek and I are just completely buddies: I love the Yankees, he loves *The Sopranos* and that's how it all started. Mutual fans. Again, we hang out at the same clubs, started talking one night, and eventually ended up going out together some times. Once, we went out to dinner with a bunch of people (including Tyra Banks and Tino Martinez) and the next day there was an article in *The New York Post* saying Tino and I were an item. We called each other, cracking up: "Okay, what's going to be next?" It was total fiction. I mean, he's happily married with three kids.

Sometimes, you almost want to have a little fun with people. Jason Cerbone and I pondered the idea of teaching the media a little lesson. Since everyone was gossiping about us being a couple (we even wound up on the *Today* show talking about it), we thought maybe we should put on a little show—really give them something to talk about. But in the end, we decided honesty was probably the best policy.

Keeping that in mind, here's the truth, the whole truth, and nothing but the truth. Derek, Jason, and Lance are all very cute and very sweet, but none are my boyfriends. I do have someone special in my life right now and he makes me *very* happy. I'm in love, and this one's for keeps. I've been through many different relationships with many different people and I've learned from all of them. There have been those love-at-first-sight ones that turn into total disasters; those friendships that blossom into something more; those crazy "set up" romances. Whether or not they lasted, whether they were good or bad, I'm glad they happened. Why? Because the more Mr. Wrongs you encounter, the easier it is to figure out who is truly your Mr. Right.

Some relationships have just not worked out for whatever reason and we're friends. If we part pals, I consider myself lucky, because I have also been through my share of hellish breakups. You know, the kind where you think you'll never get over the pain because how could you *possibly* get through a single day without this person? Well, you know what? You do get through it—and the day after, and the day after that. Life goes on. You cry your eyes out, and then suddenly you wake up one morning and realize, "What was I thinking moping over that loser? I am *so* much better off without him!" And you are. Because when he's the right one, you know it. A good relationship doesn't make you feel angry, hurt, or bad about yourself. It makes you feel excited and elated, safe and secure, all at the same time.

My mom gave me this great advice when it comes to guys: "Make your partner part of your life, but never your whole life." What that means is don't get so wrapped up in a boyfriend that you neglect what makes you "you." I had one relationship like that: I got so engrossed that nothing and no one besides him mattered to me—not friends, not family, not even myself. I was completely lost, totally pathetic, and I will never let it happen again. Never. That's not a healthy relationship. Love is about mutual respect, about appreciating someone for who he or she is on the inside and out. Your Mr. Right will make you feel like the most beautiful, intelligent, talented, and terrific person on the planet—and you give him that feeling right back. Yes, you're a couple, a team, a duo, but your team is comprised of two individuals with distinct talents and personalities. You each bring something unique and wonderful to your relationship—you shouldn't have to sacrifice any of that. Great couples complement each other and bring out the best in each other.

I know what you're thinking: "Great, Jamie, I'm

really happy you're happy. So when is this going to happen to me? When am I gonna stop dating losers and find true love?" I swear to you he or she's out there. I believe that there is someone out there for everyone—I'm a romantic that way. I'm sure that you have a "one and only" in this world, even if it takes going through a lot of "almost, but not quites" to find him. When, where? I couldn't tell you that. I certainly didn't know for myself. We all take different paths and find love at different times—it doesn't run on a schedule. And here's something else I've discovered: Just when you stop searching high and low for him, just when you're ready to throw in the towel and swear off men forever (a word of advice: nuns' habits are not very flattering), that's when it finds you.

Inquiring Minds Want to Know

It's not just press that likes to pry. Recently, I was on break from my dance rehearsals at a deli. Some guy came up to me (I had my mouth full of pickle at the time) and said, "Hey, Meadow, how's it going?" I smiled and swallowed. "Great, thanks." Then, right in the middle of my meal, he asked me to sign an autograph. I don't mind—it's actually kind of fun to be recognized—but it is strange, especially when you're not expecting it (like, in the middle of lunch).

I try to remember when I was younger and I used to *live* for those teen magazines: *Tiger Beat, Sixteen,* "Teen Hunks on Parade," whatever. I wanted to know what my favorite stars' favorite flavors of ice cream were, what underwear they had on (boxers or briefs), and if they were single or seeing someone. I ate it up. So I understand when people want to know personal things about me and I try not to get annoyed. As for the tabloids, I never take them seriously and I try not to get upset about what they write about me. How can I, when it's so ridiculous?

What does upset me is when people pass judgment without giving me the benefit of the doubt. Case in point: During *Cinderella,* I had voice trouble and I had to dash between the matinee and evening performances to see my doctor. I had just an hour before the next curtain call, so I was frantic. Some mother was standing outside Madison Square Garden with her daughter and a bunch of other moms and kids and she started screaming at me. "We've been standing here waiting for you to sign our program. How can you just walk away and disappoint all these children? What kind of person are you?" I apologized profusely. "I am so sorry, I wish I could stay, but I'm late for the doctor—I'm sick and I have to see him before the next show." The next day, she posted a vicious note on my official Web site saying I was a terrible person and a snob. Can you believe that? Every other night I stayed for hours and hours signing autographs, no matter how exhausted I was.

One night when I was in L.A. some guy cornered me outside of a club and shoved a pile of photos at me to sign. I did a few, and then said, "Sorry, that's all. I'm really exhausted, I have an early day tomorrow, and I have to leave." Well, did he give me an earful! It was clear he was just going to sell them on eBay or something, and he was mad that I wouldn't oblige. He called me names and my friends rushed me out of there.

Sometimes, people forget I'm a human being. I get tired, I get sick, and I have feelings, too. That's when the fame thing is not so fun—when people make a quick-trigger judgment about you ("You're a bitch; you're a snob"). I hate that. Because I really try so hard to be down-to-earth and approachable. I would never purposely ignore a fan or refuse an autograph—are you kidding me?

But you know what? You can't please everyone all the time, nor should you have to. And that goes for the real world as well as show business. How many times has someone rushed to make a judgment about you (or you about them)? Think about it: Could there be an explanation for someone's behavior beyond, "What a bitch! What a jerk!" You know the old, "Innocent until proven guilty?" That applies here as well. Don't call someone names until you've walked a mile in her glass slippers.

Is That Really *Me* on TV?

The first time I did a major talk show I was eighteen. Let me say that again: eighteen. It was *Good Morning America,* and I was nervous, giddy, petrified . . . all at the same time. Exactly the kind of guest a host dreads, I'd imagine, because you don't know what the heck is going to come out of her mouth or worse, she'll stare into the camera and be frozen speechless (aka Cindy Brady Syndrome). I just pictured myself being grilled by the host with those cameras zooming in, and I started to get a little jittery. Imagine giving an oral report in front of a class of *millions.* Let's see, how could I possibly embarrass myself in front of a massive amount of people in a matter of minutes? I know, go on a national news show.

Then I was booked on *The View* six months later. I had decided that I was going to "come out" about my eating disorder on the show and I was prepared for all the questions they might ask of me: Why did you do this to yourself? How bad was it? Why are you going public with it now? What I wasn't prepared for was the intense emotions I'd feel recounting my story, reliving all the pain and fear. Only a few minutes into the interview, I could feel my cheeks starting to burn and the tears welling up in my eyes. I looked out at the studio audience, and they were staring at me, pitying me. Oh, God, this was humiliating. I remember all the ladies—Joy Behar, Lisa Ling, Star Jones, and Meredith Vieira—started to cry, too. And Barbara Walters wasn't even around that day, so we couldn't blame her for making us bawl! Star grabbed my hand and held it the whole rest of the segment—she could see I was having a hard time getting through it. "Please," I pleaded with myself, "keep it together, Jamie. Don't lose it on national TV." But I couldn't help it. So much for Miss Poised and Sophisticated—I was a big cry baby.

When I came backstage, I wanted to kick myself. I remember I said to my mom and dad, "That was so bad. I was awful." And worse, who would ever want to book me on another talk show when I was such a weeper? But Lisa Ling assured me I had done a great job: "You know, Jamie," she said, "stars come on here all the time and talk about causes and charities and there's no emotion to it. You really showed how significant this cause is to you, and how it's affected you, and that's what you wanted to get across."

The more interviews I did, the better I got at it. But there were times I couldn't help acting like a little starstruck girl from Long Island (I was, after all, a little starstruck girl from Long Island). I remember when I sat down with my first publicist, she asked me what my goals were. "Well, I really want to be on *Rosie*," I said. First of all, Rosie is from Long Island where I'm from, so I love her for that. Second, she is so cool and fun and I really think she sends out a positive message to her audiences. Third, like me, she's a Broadway buff. So no offense to Dave or Jay or Conan or anyone else, Rosie was my top pick.

The publicist came through. I was booked on *Rosie* and I when I met her, I knew I had been right all along: She was great. The funny thing about talk shows is a lot of the time, you don't have a chance to meet the host before the show. So I go out there, the audience applauds, and I plop down in the chair, all smiles. I'm chatting up a storm with Rosie like we're old buddies. "How's it goin', Jamie?" "Great, Ro, how are you?" Truthfully? I had never said two words to her before in my life. You would have never known—we were simpatico for the entire segment. I was doing *Cinderella* in New York at the time, and she told me how great she thought I was and what a wonderful way it was to introduce kids to theater. I be-dazzled a *Cinderella* T-shirt for her and brought it on (Rosie collects lots of stuff, so I thought this was a good move). Later, I even did an interview about my eating disorder in her magazine.

Maybe stars are used to doing the talk show rounds and nothing about them seems out-of-the-ordinary or cool. But I was new to this; even little things impressed me! Take for example my appearance on *The Tonight Show.* I went on during the third season of *The Sopranos* which was my biggest season so far. Of course I called everyone I had ever met and told them to watch it. Never mind what I was going to say ... oh my God, what was I going I wear? You know when you're on *Tonight* you've arrived. That's how Jay Leno makes you feel: like you're special, like you're somebody. He's one person who makes a point of meeting you in the green room before the show. He shook my hand. "Thanks for coming, Jamie." I smiled. "Sure, Jay, no problem." Duh! Shouldn't I have been thanking *him* for having me on? He told me a little about what he was going to talk about, so I was totally prepared (and hopefully not nervous). But the best thing about *The Tonight Show?* The Jay Bar. What, you ask, is that? It's a huge rolling cart that comes around with candy, alcohol, soda, any snack you could possibly imagine. Potato chips. Got 'em. Gummi Bears? Right there. Diet soda? No prob. It's the coolest thing you've ever seen.

Jay also likes to have fun. We talked a lot about how the *Sopranos* gang likes to kid around on the set (food fights!), and how silly and light the atmosphere is all the time. I told stories of how there were always bloopers you never saw on screen. Like the time I did a scene in a car: The first take, I broke a nail; the second, I slammed my foot in the door; the third time, I got out and tripped. The audience roared with laughter; Jay roared with laughter. Hey, I thought, I'm doing pretty well, here. I can be funny. I can be charming. I didn't cry once.

The only weird thing—and this goes for any talk show—is that you don't really know where to look while you're telling your story. Do you look at Jay? The camera? The audience that's laughing at your jokes? My head was going in every direction. It's amazing I didn't get whiplash.

Some interviewers, however, don't want yuks (mental note: no food-fight stories, Jamie). You're supposed to be a serious source for a serious interview. Like the time I did *Oprah*. She asked me to record a little message that she then aired on her show. Thursday is Spirit Day, and I talked about how I keep my spirit after my eating disorder and how I deal. Or *Good Morning America*. Diane Sawyer interviewed me. I remember a lot of friends saying to me afterwards, "Wow, you really handled yourself well with her." I know people think of her as a tough journalist, but I wasn't the slightest bit intimidated. She treated me like an adult. I wasn't really worried about the interview, because I was simply speaking from my heart and my experiences. Diane was really nice to me and very compassionate.

The surest way to beat talk show anxiety is to use

the buddy system: You bring a pal with you. Jason Cerbone and I did the *Today* show together after the season three finale when Jackie, Jr., is bumped off. It was crazy. *The New York Post* ran a picture of him from the show in a coffin with the headline "Jack in a Box," and all the rumors about us dating in real life were flying *(Page 6* reported we were all over each other at a bar). So we went on *Today* to set the record straight with Matt Lauer. Our publicists were like, "Just go on and be yourselves and squash all those stupid stories." So we did. We had so much fun joking around with Matt. "So the rumor is you two are canoodling," he pried. Jason and I looked at each other and shrugged. We didn't even know what "canoodling" meant, so how could we be doing it?

I also had a great time on *Politically Incorrect,* and I was very concerned at first that I'd come off sounding stupid. Bill Maher is an absolute sweetheart. He said to me before the show, "Listen, don't get upset if I disagree with you, because that's what I do on this show. That's my job." I was like, "Okay, I'm just going to give you my honest opinion and hope I don't stick my foot in my mouth." The subject was school shootings, and it was me, Bill, Howie Mandel, and two students from Columbine and Santee. I went with my gut and I think I came out sounding halfway intelligent. The good thing was, I didn't have time to stress beforehand—the two high school kids were really nervous, so I was busy trying to calm them down before we went on air. How do you like that? There I was, telling these two teens that being interviewed on TV is no biggie. "You'll be great. It's so easy if you just learn to relax and be yourself." I guess I have learned to do that—and that's even cooler than the Jay Bar.

7

Head Games

Rarely do I open a menu and think, "Hmmm, what am I in the mood for today?" Instead, it's more like, "What can I eat? What's the healthier choice?" I see my best friend order a greasy burger and fries without contemplating "Should I/Shouldn't I?" and I'm jealous. I want to be able to eat whatever appeals without stressing over it. I'm working hard on that. Just this weekend I ate fast food—this may not be a big deal for you, but it is for me. I'm active; I know I can burn it off. But eating, say, a Big Mac, is not something I can do easily, not without justifying it first. ("Hey, I ate healthy all week long and exercised so I'm entitled to splurge a little.")

Anyone who tells you that you "get over" an eating disorder has never had one. I'll always struggle with weight and food issues, it's just that now, I'm aware of them and I don't feel like they're controlling me. Instead, I'm controlling them. But the business that I am in doesn't make it easy. It's hard to keep a healthy perspective on your body when the whole world is watching— and critiquing. Because you're a public figure, people think they have the right to nitpick and scrutinize everything about you: a bad hair day, a zit on your chin, even PMS bloat. Why do people in the media think they have the right to judge us?

Part of it, I believe, is jealousy. They think, "Hey, if I knock her down, I'll look bigger." But I have feelings, too. I'm human. Why should I have to live up to someone else's ideal? So what if I'm not some stick figure. Like J. Lo sings, "I'm real." Excuse me . . . I'm Cuban. Even when I was really skinny I had an ass, and I'm always gonna have it. Part of my stage show is a dance number that we do to this song called "Baby Got Back" which is about having a big butt. In the beginning it's my dancers saying it to me—kind of poking fun at it. And you know what? There's nothing wrong with it. It works for J. Lo— she shakes her booty and flaunts her curves. So there you go—be proud of your "assets," no matter what size they are.

I know it's easier said than done. Especially when

98

someone launches a sneak attack and torpedoes your self-confidence. I was at a photo shoot a few years ago for a teen magazine, and this guy stylist went through the rack of clothes and said to me, "Honey, are you *sure* you wear this size?" He was insinuating, of course, that I didn't *look* like I wore that small a size. Ouch. Flashback to the "fat comments" from *Sopranos* fans online and even that day on the beach when I felt like Gargantua next to my ex's ex. That's all it took. The whole shoot, I felt horrible about myself. I remember my friend Sloane was there, and she kept telling me how beautiful my hair and makeup looked, trying to make me feel better and to distract me from thinking about his snide remark. It didn't work. The only thing running through my head was "Oh my God, I must be *huge!*" I felt so ugly. It ruined my day. It ruined my week.

But you know what? When I got the pictures back, I didn't look ugly at all—I looked great. And I learned something from it: I had no one to blame for the way I felt except myself. I should *never* have let anyone make me feel that way. Why did I let a few nasty words shatter my self-esteem?

Like I said, Aida Turturro is my role model. She never lets anyone influence her body image. Because she loves herself, people are not looking at her and thinking what size she is, they're thinking, "This is such an awesome lady. She's so much fun to be around." Or take someone like Emme. I met her at an UNO party and I told her I really admire her for setting such a great example. She's proven to the world that "beautiful" comes in all shapes and sizes—and you should embrace the person you are, inside and out.

These are the women that I strive to be like because they don't let people define who they are or hold them back. They write their own rules—I think that's amazing. The greatest accomplishment in the world is figuring out who you are and being true to that person.

So how do you build your confidence and prevent some jerk from walking all over it? The more aware you are of what it is that motivates these toxic types (jealousy, insecurity, a serious attitude problem), the better armed you'll be the next time it happens. I feel sorry for people who have to put others down to build themselves up; they're sad. And let me tell you, it doesn't make any difference if you're on a TV show or magazine covers or on MTV—people still take shots at you. The thing is, you can't let yourself be an easy target. If you feel good about yourself, that really comes through, and nobody can take that away from you. In fact, they won't even try.

Wanna see what I mean? You walk into a room thinking, "I feel good about myself; I'm happy" and you just watch what a magnet you are. You give off positive energy that people are drawn to. But the reverse is also true: You can have on the hottest outfit in the world that costs thousands of dollars and if you don't feel good about yourself, you'll look terrible in it. I'm telling you, forget the Fendi bag: Confidence is the best accessory. It can make or break your look.

And of course, the reverse works as well. If you hate who you are, then that projects, too. I look at my prom pictures, and I look really unhappy. I remember that night my hair didn't turn out the way I wanted it to and instead of just letting it go, I dwelled on it. It's so clear in the photos—here's Jamie, hating her hair. I guess those pictures are a good reminder for me: Get over it, girl!

I'm not a size 0 and that's okay. I'd prefer it if girls would look at me and say, "Hey, she looks like I do. She's got a butt and hips." It took me a while to realize this, that I don't have to fit into a category or be a certain type (i.e. skinny actress with big boobs and not a bit of cellulite on her). I'm an actress, a singer, a dancer—that's my job. I have to be strong and remember where I've been and that I could easily slip back there again.

I actually wish I was better at speaking up—I avoid conflicts at all costs and I know that's terrible. I need to stand up for myself more, but when I do, I feel like a bitch. I guess there's a right way to do it, a happy medium between being sweet and passive and going ballistic. I'm working on it because I believe you should assert yourself. You don't have to be a bitch, but you shouldn't be a pushover either.

Cover Girl

The media is so hung up on the whole weight issue, but they contradict themselves. One week, a cover will have an actress talking about her great new diet and how you can use it to lose pounds, then the next week, they're complaining she's too thin. What's right? And is it really anybody's business? It does come up in my interviews: "What are your fitness and diet tips?" Sometimes I want to say—and sometimes I *do* say—"You know, that's irrelevant." Why don't they ask me my advice on how we can achieve world peace—now that's important. Does everyone really need to know what I ate for breakfast last Tuesday?

It kind of puzzles me how all of these magazines tell you how to get fab abs overnight or lose twenty pounds in a week. First of all, that's just not gonna happen—even if you're doing a gazillion crunches the night before, you're not waking up with a flat stomach if you didn't have one to begin with. Everything is about slimming down and toning up (a girl can start to feel like a yo-yo with all those ups and downs). But maybe instead of telling women to lose weight, the message needs to be "get healthy." And "healthy" is different for everyone: For some people, it means starting an exercise program to get your heart pumping and cutting back on the junk food. For me, it meant *not* starving myself to death and accepting who I am. There are a lot of really positive young role models out there, Drew Barrymore and Kate Winslet and others who've basically said, "I don't care if I don't fit the mold, I'm happy with the way I am." Maybe instead of weight-loss articles, magazines should run more stories on how to boost your self-esteem and love your body (I could have really used that).

Another thing you have to know: What you're seeing in these magazines—pictures of women with not an inch of fat or flab and perfect bodies—are totally fake. Every image is retouched. Do you know how many times I have gone to a shoot and had some photographer or art director tell me, "Don't worry about that, Jamie. We'll fix it later." Sometimes you wind up looking more like a mannequin than a human being. Don't get me wrong—the photos are almost always amazing and I love them—but sometimes it's refreshing to see a Polaroid of the real thing before some retoucher works wonders on it.

You'd be really shocked to see what some of these

actresses and supermodels look like for real. I doubt anyone has flawless skin, no wrinkles, and gravity-defying boobs (unless they're fake ones!). Those pictures are pretty to look at, but you should never hold them up as a symbol of what you aspire to be. There's a lot that goes on to get these women to look that good. I know this, because I have been primped, tucked, taped, brushed, and painted for hours at shoots. And I'll admit it: I don't wake up in the morning looking like I do in a magazine or on TV. No one does.

I've done a lot of shoots (*Rolling Stone, Rosie* magazine, *Self, Seventeen, Teen People, CosmoGirl, Latina*), but I got the strongest reactions to my *Maxim* cover. Okay, I guess I should have known that people would be shocked by it. I wore a gold lamé tank showing my stomach and tight hot pants with a gold gun on them. Then there are shots of me in this low-cut minidress and high heels and a couple of bikini tops. It was the first time people were seeing me grown-up, looking like a woman and not a little girl. I have on this really smoky, glamorous makeup, too. So yes, it caused a bit of a stir because it's not how people think of me or Meadow.

Sometimes when you do a shoot like that, people assume you're trying to make a statement: "Okay, I want to be a sex bomb . . ." But it wasn't that way for me. *Pullease!* I am so *not* a sex bomb (my friends, no doubt, are either nodding their heads in agreement right now or laughing hysterically). You should see me on a regular day: sweatshirt, jeans, a bandana covering my hair. How sexy is that? I knew what I was getting into by agreeing to this cover; I knew the kind of photos that *Maxim* runs. I thought it would be fun to try something a little different. I didn't think this was "the new me." In the end, I don't think it even looked like me (I was so tan and oily). It was a fantasy, and that's what all magazine covers truly are. The only dangerous thing is when you start believing they're real—and that anything less than the perfection they present is unacceptable. The little flaws we have are what make us special and unique. You can airbrush them out all you want, but I'm glad to wake up with mine in the morning.

8

Mission Impossible

How happy was I? *The Sopranos* was a *huge* hit; I was getting all sorts of offers (magazine covers, movies, talk shows, you name it); I was planning on recording an album and maybe even doing a musical. Life couldn't be better.

So of course, it had to get worse. We had just wrapped the second season of *The Sopranos* in June 2000 and I was expected to start shooting season three in August. In between, I filmed a dinky little independent film in the wooded areas of New Jersey. The location was literally in the middle of nowhere—nothing for miles around but trees, bushes and bugs—can you say "tick city?" So when we wrapped, I joked, "You guys, we should all probably go get checked for Lyme disease." Of course, I didn't take my own advice seriously—I didn't see any tick bites on me (those little rings they warn you about), so I didn't bother.

I went home, and two weeks later I had to go to Canada to do some promo work for *The Sopranos*. The show had just started airing there and they needed the cast to do interviews, appearances, and stuff. I woke up early, put on my sneakers, and went for a walk with my mom. Only a few minutes into it, I had to stop. I told my mom, "You know, I think I tied my sneaker on my right foot too tight. It feels like it's cutting off the circulation." So I took my shoe off, but it didn't seem to help. I had this kind of tingly numb sensation—like pins and needles or when your foot falls asleep. Mom was a little concerned (aren't moms always?), but I was the opposite. I'm the anti-hypochondriac. So I chalked it up to a pinched nerve and put it out of my head. *Whatever*...

I went the whole day doing all these interviews for TV, radio, and print. By the time I got home at night, the numbness had spread from my foot all the way up to my calf. The next day, my other foot started to feel numb, too. Now *this* was weird. But I kept ignoring it—I had a lot of plans and I wasn't going to let some little pinched nerve interrupt them.

After Canada, I flew to Florida to visit a boyfriend. Every morning I was there, I noticed the numbness climbing up my legs higher and higher. I didn't want to bug my boyfriend's parents about it, so I just pretended everything was fine. But by the third day, it had gone all the way up to my butt. It's hard to explain how it felt. Imagine picture poking your foot with a needle and not being able to feel pain, just a slight touch. Or holding a cold spoon against your leg and not being able to sense the cold. All of a sudden, my legs started getting a little heavy, too. At this point, I mentioned it to my boyfriend's family. His mom was so nice—she massaged my legs and suggested I soak in the Jacuzzi, trying to soothe it. They asked me if I was okay and I said, "Yeah, it's no biggie." I stayed the whole visit and never really complained, so nobody thought it was anything serious.

At the airport, waiting for my flight home, I called my parents and mentioned my mysterious numbness. They were really mad that I had been neglecting this (and hiding it from them), but I said I was fine, "Just send someone to pick me up at the airport when I land." My dad said he'd have a car service waiting and I boarded my flight. I fell asleep on the plane, and when I woke up three hours later, I could barely move my legs. I struggled to stand up, but I didn't want to ask anyone for help (way too embarrassing). Somehow, I managed to get my bag and slowly made it from the gate to where the driver was waiting for me. What should have taken five minutes took me a half an hour, because my legs were like lead and each step was agony. In the car going home, I sobbed on the phone to my dad. "Something is wrong with me!"

My dad helped me out of the car and into our house, and I sat down to have a drink of water before we went to the hospital. At that point, my legs completely gave out. I couldn't stand back up; I couldn't budge them an inch; I couldn't walk or even wiggle my toes. I was terrified and so furious at myself for letting it get this far. What had I done?

My dad scooped me up in his arms like I was a baby and carried me into the car. He drove us to the emergency room of Long Island Hospital. He's amazing in a crisis—calm, strong, and clear-headed. My poor mom was as terrified and as hysterical as I was, so we decided it would be better if she waited at home. We'd call her when we had any answers.

Test Anxiety

The first thing they did when I got to the hospital was ask my dad, "Do you mind if we give your daughter a pregnancy test?" My mouth fell open. Hello? People, this is my *father* and this is totally humiliating! He took it in stride; he was too worried to even react to the possibility that his little girl could be having S-E-X: "Sure, whatever you need to do." I, on the other hand, was mortified. "Trust me," I told the nurses, "I am so *not* pregnant." Nonetheless, they wheeled me off to go give a urine sample. When I got back to the ER waiting room, I fell asleep.

I woke up two hours later to find all these doctors hovering over me. "Can you feel this? Can you feel that? Can you wiggle your toes?" They were poking the bottoms of my feet with needles, twisting, pulling, and bending my legs into every position you can think of. I felt like a rubber band, not a person. "No, I can't," I said. "I can't feel anything. I can't move at all." From the doctors' worried expressions I could tell this was no pinched nerve.

The numbness was now up to my stomach, and it was starting to affect my breathing—I felt like a weight was lying on my chest. They doctors threw out the words "Guillain-Barré syndrome" and I saw my dad's face go white. I'd heard of Guillain-Barré before, and I knew it involved paralysis and could be life-threatening, but I just couldn't let my mind go there. Even while everyone scratched their heads and poked me, I kept believing, "Okay, they'll eventually just figure it out, give me some medicine, and I can go home in a few hours."

Unfortunately, it wasn't that simple. Long Island Hospital decided I needed to see specialists and rushed me by ambulance over to Manhassett Hospital. When I got there, there were more tests: CT scans, MRIs, more doctors prodding me from head to toe. But I wasn't panicking. In fact, I think my emotions were as numb as my lower body. My dad says I was just lying in bed, staring at the ceiling, not saying a word, with tears streaming down my face.

The tests went all night long, and by 7 A.M. I was starving. Of course, no one would let me eat anything—they had more tests scheduled and they required an empty stomach. So now I was hungry, cranky, *and* exhausted—not a good combination. Somehow, I managed to doze, and when I woke up again in the ICU, there was a brand new huddle of doctors peering down at me with furrowed brows.

"Can you feel this? Can you wiggle your toes?" Here we go again! By now, I was sick of the same questions over and over, and frustrated that I was getting no answers. So that was it; I lost it: "NO I CAN'T FEEL ANYTHING!" I screamed. "WOULD YOU PEOPLE JUST LEAVE ME ALONE?" The head doctor, Dr. Hamovic, was very nice and very understanding. "Jamie," he said, "I know you're upset and scared and that you hate this, but we have to ask these things so we can help you."

He then told me he had to give me a spinal tap—which I knew, from *ER* and all those other medical dramas, involved a needle in your back. "Why? Why? Don't do that to me! I don't want it!" I was crying hysterically and my parents (my mom had come to the hospital at this point) were trying desperately to calm me down and tell me it would be all right. My mom stayed with me while Dr. Hamovic did the procedure. I felt the initial pain of the needle going in, but it actually wasn't as bad as I thought it was going to be. The doctor was an expert, and he was able to draw a lot of spinal fluid without hurting me much at all.

They then put me on steroids to keep the numbness from rising while they waited for the test results to come in. For five days, there was no improvement, and the first tests didn't seem to indicate there was anything wrong. My test for Lyme disease came back negative, so the doctors ruled that out. "You have to be patient," Dr. Hamovic told me. "We're going to find out what's wrong, I promise you."

In the meantime, it was "Let's Cheer Up Jamie" week with all my friends and family filling my room with flowers, candy, stuffed animals, and get-well balloons and cards. Though I appreciated the visits and good wishes, the steroids caused vicious mood swings, and I would yell, cry, even throw things without warning. I once screamed at my dad for not stacking a pile of magazines the way I wanted them. People would joke: "Be careful going in there. You never know when she might turn into Linda Blair from *The Exorcist.* ..."

Everyone took shifts staying with me. My brother Brian was amazing. He came every morning at 6 A.M.

because he knew I'd wake up at that time, and he'd sit with me through the afternoon and watch my soap opera, *Passions* (you just gotta love all those campy characters who live in Harmony). After school, my friends would come. It's funny, you learn who your real friends are when something like this happens. People I thought for sure would come to see me, didn't. At first that made me mad, but now I understand it. Sometimes people just don't want to deal with other people's problems. Or maybe they're uncomfortable with the situation: They don't know what to say so it's easier to ignore it.

There were, however, great friends who really reached out to me during this tough time—my friend Lindsey, for one. She came every single night. And when we informed the *Sopranos* team of what was going on, David Chase, Edie, and Ilene Landress (one of the co-executive producers) all came to the hospital. I told everyone the same thing: "This is just temporary. As soon as they figure out what's causing it, I am *so* outta here!" My parents were glad I was keeping my spirits up, and they tried to pretend that they shared my optimism. But once, my dad was stroking my hair and I looked up into his eyes and saw he was crying. It broke my heart; the last thing in the world I wanted to do was hurt him. Hadn't I hurt my parents enough with my eating disorder? I felt like a rotten daughter, but my dad reassured me: "You're the best daughter in the whole world."

My family also didn't want me to know that the prognosis wasn't looking good. I overheard my dad whispering with a doctor in the hall. "We really don't know what it is," the doctor was saying. "We have to be honest with you. There is a possibility that she will never walk again." Hearing that, I should have been depressed; I should have been frightened. But at that moment, the only thought running through my head was "No, you're wrong. I *will* walk."

I'd be lying if I said there weren't a few moments, especially when the hospital room was dark and quiet and my dad was dozing in the chair nearby, when I felt frightened, moments when I thought, "What if . . ." What if I was facing a future in a wheelchair? What if this was the end of all I had worked so hard for? What about *The Sopranos?* What about my career? What about my *life?* But I'd force those thoughts out of my mind, almost like I was slamming a door shut on them. A voice inside me shouted, "Jamie, it doesn't matter what the doctors say, you know better." Maybe it was the angel on my shoulder telling me so; maybe it was just me being stubborn. But whatever it was, I wasn't ready to give up.

At Long Last, an Answer

My grandma and my mom were going to church every day, lighting candles and praying for me. Grandma even told God she'd give up chocolate for six months if he'd just make me well again. "Oh, Jamie," my mom would sigh, "I wish this was happening to me, not to you." My parents would say that over and over again. I think as hard as this was on me, it was twice as hard on them. Then out of the blue, one of my friend's mom who was a doctor made a suggestion. Dr. Taff said, "You know, I think I saw something like this once before. Let's test Jamie again for Lyme." They sent out my blood work to a different lab, and this time, it came back 85 percent positive for Lyme. Hooray! Finally some explanation for what was going on.

The doctors took that result and ran with it. They yanked me off the steroids and put me on a strong course of antibiotics via IV. That wasn't so bad, but in order to prevent cramping and blood clots in my legs, I had to have a shot in my stomach three times a day. I cried for an hour after every injection. In the middle of all this, a reporter from some trashy tabloid showed up at the hospital asking me for an interview. I was like, "Are you kidding me? Get out of my face!"

We couldn't release a statement because we didn't know what I had, but that didn't stop the tabloid from running a horrible story: "*Sopranos* Star Dying!" My dad tried to hide it from me when it came out because he thought I'd be upset, but actually, I thought it was funny. The only info they could get was from some nurse. The reporter overheard her saying that I hadn't had a bowel movement that day, so the tabloid interpreted that as "Sigler is having trouble with her bowels." Like I was dying of constipation or something. It was so stupid I had to laugh. At least the picture they used of me was good.

The day after they started me on the antibiotics, the doctors came in to check on me. It had now been seven days of paralysis. "How do you feel, Jamie?" You know, I actually felt pretty good. Then they asked, "Can you do *something* for us?" And just like that, I wiggled my toes. "Hallelujah!" They took me out of ICU and put me into a regular hospital room and I started physical therapy. Every day was that much better and I was fighting that much harder. I had to use a walker at first, but after two days I was walking on my own. I remember my mom came one night, and I told her to stand at the door. "Look what I can do," I said, and I walked right to her and fell into her arms. She cried and hugged me—it was like a baby taking her first steps to her mother.

For the next five days, I kept begging the doctors and nurses, "I want to get out of here. I'm good to go." Finally, they gave me my walking papers . . . literally. I went home and I have never been so glad to see my bedroom, my kitchen, my neighborhood. It was like everything looked, smelled, and tasted so awesome. In a lot of ways, it was like being reborn—I appreciated everything so much more, every little detail of my life, especially the way the floor felt under my bare feet. After crying for so long, all I could do now was smile. My cheeks started to hurt!

It took a while for my strength to come back, and I had to continue with the antibiotics (I had an IV I had to hook myself up to at home once a day for three weeks) and physical therapy. I noticed that when I got on a bike I couldn't pedal very far, and in the shower, I couldn't stand too long. My legs got tired and I had sit on a little stool. I wanted to bounce back right away, but my body was saying, "Slow down there, Jamie, this is going to take time." It was so hard to be patient, but I don't think I ever complained. I was just so thrilled to be back and standing on my own two feet again. Little by little, my strength returned and I was back to normal. In August, I started shooting *The Sopranos* and never had to miss a single day of work.

It's funny, even after this terrible ordeal, I never thought, "Oh, poor Jamie!" I never really felt that way, even during the hardest most painful parts. I never pitied myself or got mad at God for letting this happen to me. I just accepted that it was something that I had to get through and I *would* get through. And I'd walk away (yes *walk* away) having learned something valuable. What did I learn? First of all, don't ever take anything for granted; just being able to wiggle your toes when you wake up in the morning is a miracle. Second, when the odds are stacked against you, don't lose faith. Nothing is impossible. There's this great song in *Cinderella:* "The world is made of zanies and fools/Who don't believe in sensible rules/And don't believe what sensible people say/Impossible things are happening every day!"

9

A Whole New Tune

Right after New Year's 2001, things really took off. I finished the third season of *The Sopranos* in February, and literally two days later, I hit the road for a thirty-nine-city tour of Rodgers and Hammerstein's *Cinderella*. Theater has always been my first love, so the idea of doing this musical—which included my Broadway debut at the Theater at Madison Square Garden—was an offer I couldn't refuse. My mom and I spotted the casting call in the *Backstage* magazine classifieds. I was eager to get back to doing theater, and it sounded fun. I called my manager and said, "I want to go in on this."

The casting people were interested, but they asked if I wouldn't mind auditioning. I had *The Sopranos* on my resumé, but that didn't mean I could carry a tune. I said, "Sure, no problem." I did a song and read some scenes. They asked me if I could ballroom dance. Visions of Fred and Ginger came to mind. "You mean like waltz?" I asked. "Um, not really. But I'm a quick learner!" They must have believed me, because a week later they called to say I had the job.

The first half of the tour conflicted with my *Sopranos* schedule, so they worked it out so I could split the tour with another Cinderella. She turned out to be Deborah Gibson, whom I *loved* when I was younger (I used to wear her perfume, Electric Youth, and had all her records back when she was Debbie Gibson). When she was rehearsing in New York, I used to go in, hang with her and the cast, and watch them so I could get a feel for the show. Before long, *The Sopranos* wrapped, and it was my turn to slip on the glass slippers (they're actually plastic, but don't tell anyone).

Talk about a fairytale come true: Every night, I got to come down the staircase of the palace in that gorgeous gown and dance with Prince Charming (you wouldn't believe how good I got at that waltz). I made so many great friends in the cast, especially my fairy godmother, Eartha Kitt. What a dynamo she is. She's seventy-five years old, and most mornings, she was dragging my ass to go work out with her. To be totally honest, I didn't really know who she was when I first met her. I mean, I saw her once as Catwoman in the old *Batman* reruns, but I had no idea what an incredible life and career she's had. She is full of stories. She speaks seven languages, she's traveled the world, and she takes a stand on so many political issues. I was in awe of her. "Eartha, when I'm your age," I'd tell her, "I would be happy if I had just half your wisdom and your passion for life."

The thing I loved most about *Cinderella* (besides singing those beautiful classic songs that Julie Andrews once performed on stage) was meeting the little kids in the audience. No matter how tired I was, I would spend hours after the show signing autographs. I knew what that was like when I used to go see shows, how much it meant to me to talk to an actor at the stage door. Meeting these kids all over the country was wonderful, but New York was the tour stop I was looking forward to the most. Not only was it my hometown, but it was Broadway, my lifelong dream.

Now, after reading this book so far, you must be familiar with Jamie's Law: "If something can go wrong, it will . . . usually at the most inopportune moment."

The morning of our opening night, I came down with severe laryngitis. I couldn't speak a word. My vocal chords simply had been pushed to their limit. On the road, we were doing eight shows a week (in New York, we upped that number to eleven), so after belting my little heart out from coast to coast, I was left with nothing more than a croak. I raced to the doctor and he gave me a shot. I was steaming my throat all day long and drinking warm liquids, trying desperately to cure myself in time for curtain. It was a miracle that when I opened my mouth to sing "In My Own Little Corner" (my first solo) the notes came out. My castmates looked stunned as well as relieved—I think they were a little worried Cinderella would have to be performing her role in mime that night! To ensure this didn't happen again, I had to keep my mouth shut most of the day before every performance (sheer torture for me—I usually have a cell phone glued to my ear). Thankfully, this story had a happily ever after: I got through the rest of the tour without too much trouble.

I Want My MTV

In October of 2001, around the time we were about to start filming the fourth season of *The Sopranos,* my record, *Here to Heaven,* came out (the record company first heard me singing on *The Sopranos).* The title of the CD was actually the title of a song that never made it on to the album. That's bizarre, I know, but I am terrible at coming up with titles. This sounded pretty and seemed to reflect my spirituality, so what the heck!

The fact that the title made little sense kind of goes with the whole process of recording the album. The whole thing was poorly planned. It took a year to make because of the million other things I was doing. The label would send me songs and I would just go into a studio whenever I had a free moment (mostly in New York, some times in Seattle when we doing *Cinderella*, once in Miami) and lay down vocals. I was impatient; the label was impatient. In retrospect, not enough thought went into it. Which isn't to say it's a *bad* album—I just don't think any of us ever considered if it really captured my style, or if it distinguished me in any way from all the other young female singers out there. Once it was made, it was just a bunch of good songs that anyone could have sung. It didn't have anything about it that reflected who I was.

Unfortunately, I knew nothing about the recording industry, so I let the "experts" guide me, even against my better judgment sometimes. It bit me in the ass in the end. But that's what happens. You have these experiences and you grow from them. There are so many artists who release several albums before ever making one that made it big. Take Janet Jackson: She recorded three albums before *Control* made her a star. I'm still trying to find my style. I don't think it's pop—I'm not Britney or Mandy or Christina. I like the slow songs the best. I'm a balladeer—that comes from my theater roots. I prefer singing with emotion and acting out a song, not just strutting around. But I guess I fit the mold for what the label initially wanted: their own pop princess. And look, I can try and pull it off, but it's just not me. Even the cover wasn't what I had in mind.

When I got to the shoot, the stylist handed me a bikini. "Why don't you try this on?" I looked at this flimsy little thing. "Why? What does that have to do with my album?" After posing in several other outfits, the bikini was brought up again. "Just take one shot in it," the stylist pleaded. You know that if you do that "one" shot they could wind up using it, but I agreed to put it on with a skirt over it. Thankfully, that photo didn't make it on to the cover, but the picture they chose was not my favorite, either. I like the one inside the CD liner; the label wanted something more "smoldery." The label had the final say, not me—and this was *my* album, *my* name. I was so not happy.

Regardless of how it turned out, I was going to promote it. I had worked hard—a lot of people had—and I wanted it to sell. At first, it was very exciting, especially my first single "Cry Baby" debuting on *TRL*. You have to understand, only two years ago, I was standing outside MTV's New York studios in Times Square screaming my head off with about a million other crazed kids. My friend Cathy was in love with the Backstreet Boys and insisted that we take the train into the city to see them on

TRL. So now, here I was on that very same program, sitting in the green room backstage about to go out and chat with Carson Daly. That's a little freaky . . .

I'd been on MTV several times before—even hosted a New Year's Eve special for them—so I shouldn't have been nervous. But this was something totally new—a different side of me that I was showing to audiences. I wondered if people would like me as a singer as well as an actress. At least I had my posse of supporters in the green room: my cousins Jackie and Brett; A.J. and his partner, Bobby; Stephen Baldwin, the actor, who is A.J.'s buddy; and a little girl, Danielle, whom I used to do shows with and her friend from school (I knew being backstage at MTV would be a *major* deal for them, so I told them to come).

Carson introduced me and I came out to everyone applauding. He is so laid-back and easy-going. He makes it feel like you're talking to a friend, not doing an interview. Totally no pressure or stress. Stephen did this joke where he sat in the audience and held up cue cards that said silly things. Then they showed a clip of my video for "Cry Baby." The video was actually great. Nigel Dick directed it, and he made it a wonderful experience for me. He's known for imaging people and really capturing who they are. He's worked with everyone from Britney to Backstreet to Guns N' Roses. I loved how fun and happy-go-lucky the concept was—

just a bunch of young girls running around having a good time. We shot it in Pasadena in less than twenty-four hours. What a blast! You pull up to a set and know everything and everyone is there for you. I felt like such the diva!

After *TRL* we raced across the street and I performed live at the Virgin Megastore in Times Square. There were hundreds of people lined up to see me (gulp) and buy the CD. My cousin Jackie said. "This is *wild.*" And it was. I had only three days to rehearse three of my songs, one with a complicated dance routine (my choreographer, Trey, and his assistant, Sadie, were my "backup" dancers trying to make me look good). I had no idea what I was going to wear that day—everything was planned at the last minute. So you can understand how really glad I was when it was all over and I could relax. I went backstage and hugged all the people who turned out to see me: my cousins and my aunt, my mom and grandma, my brothers, my friend Lindsey and her sister, even my friend Jonathan who goes to Columbia took the subway down. Afterwards, I was autographing posters and CD covers when I heard this voice: "Could ya write, 'To Drea'?" It was Drea de Mateo, and she'd heard I was going to be at Virgin and came to surprise me. She even bought a CD!

So that was the start of the whirlwind that eventually turned into a full-fledged tornado. In all the excitement, I was running myself ragged making appearances. I know that's what happens when you're starting out—the idea is to "put yourself out there" and create a buzz. You have to work hard to succeed. But no one says you have to establish your entire music career in three weeks. I was literally in a new place every day. Sometimes I'd wake up in the morning and go, "Okay, what city am I in?" I'd do a club appearance at 1 A.M. then a radio show at 6. This is what it feels like to be a pop star, right? Wrong. And I should have known better. I remember turning to A.J. at one point and saying, "I don't feel well, and something bad is going to happen if I don't slow down a little." He was totally cool with it: "Then just say 'no,' Jamie." But I didn't. It was just "one more interview, one more appearance, one more city . . ." until what I feared the most happened.

One particularly hectic day, I had a photo shoot in the morning, then an interview, then a rehearsal, then a sound check for a performance later that night. I had been going nonstop from 7 A.M. till 5 P.M. with barely a second to catch my breath. I came home to my apartment. I had half an hour to change to go to a benefit dinner. My mom, my brother, and A.J. were in my living room waiting for me. I went into the bathroom and I felt lousy. I threw up, then I kind of crumpled on the floor. Oh my god . . . not again. *I couldn't stand up.*

This time, I went crazy. "I don't want to go through

this again," I sobbed. "I can't. I warned everyone. I knew this would happen." They took me to the hospital. "Jamie, we know what it is." My mom tried to calm me down. "They'll just put you on the antibiotics again and you'll be fine." At the hospital, we gave the doctors my whole history. They nodded, then ordered a spinal tap—and this time, they wouldn't let my mom stay with me and hold my hand. They numbed my spine first and they asked me if I could feel anything. "No, it's fine, it's good." I replied. I just wanted to get it over with. But I wasn't completely numb, and when they put the needle in, the pain was excruciating. It felt like an electric shock went through me; my body literally jumped a foot in the air. My mom was in the hallway and heard me scream—she said it sounded like they were killing me. "We're so sorry . . ." the doctors said, and I could feel them cleaning the blood off my back. "We'll come back in a half hour and try it again." It was the worst pain I have ever felt, and I was begging for drugs, *something* to make it go away. But they didn't give it to me, and the next try was just as bad. "That's it!" I screamed. "No more. You're not doing this again. You'll do it tomorrow, I want to sleep."

So my mom slept there with me and I woke up in the morning to another round of doctors asking me the same questions all over again. I couldn't stand it: I was right back where I had been five months ago. But this time, I wasn't that helpless little girl in the bed anymore. I was pissed. I was working so hard, and this just wasn't fair. I felt like my body was betraying me. "They told me I was better," I insisted. "So why did it come back?" Again, the doctors had no answers, but they suspected that all the stress and lack of rest had knocked my immune system for a loop.

An MRI showed lesions on my spine which had come from the Lyme. "We need to do a tap," said one doctor who was very nice. "And I promise you, we'll give you something so it won't hurt." They gave me a shot of morphine and I began to get groggy. A.J.'s other clients, the guys from LMNT, had come to visit me and they said I was talking pretty funny, like I was drunk. "How's that?" the doctor asked. I was paranoid that it would hurt, so I lied and said I needed more morphine. That's the last thing I remember: I never felt the tap. I don't even remember them doing it. I slept for a day.

I woke up hooked up to another IV. My dad brought me pizza, and I was actually in good spirits, joking around. As soon as the antibiotics kicked in, my legs came back. After five days, the hospital released me and I was okay. In the meantime, my label was itching to get me back on the road. So three days after I got out of the hospital, I was on a plane to London to promote my album overseas. Practically the minute we landed, I felt sick, like I was coming down with flu or something. I wound up with severe sinusitus and a high fever, so forget the promotional: I was in bed the whole time we were in England. "That's it," I told A.J. "I don't care if the label gets mad. My health is so much more important than this crap. From now on, that's my top priority—not selling CDs."

And I mean that. It took going through this Lyme hell twice to learn that lesson (once might have been enough for most girls, but not me. I have to come back for seconds). My label here in the U.S. shut down, and now I have this great European label that I love. They know how to handle me, and they remixed all my music.

Over here, I'll just rethink it. I'm not in a rush. I'm shopping around for a new label. I'll get back into a studio when it's right and when I find the right music. Like Janet Jackson, "I'm in control."

10

What I Know Now

This is the last chapter of my book. So how come it doesn't feel like an ending? Maybe that's because in so many ways, I still have a lot of journeying ahead of me. There's this great song from *Bye Bye Birdie*, "I've Got a Lot of Living to Do." Well, that's how I feel. If all this has happened to me and I'm only twenty-one, I can't even imagine what lies ahead.

Interviewers are always asking me, "So, Jamie, where do you see yourself ten years from now?" As if I could gaze into some crystal ball and see the future! What am I supposed to say, "Gee, I'd like to win an Oscar, a Tony, and a Grammy? Or maybe costar with

Tom Cruise?" All of the above would be cool—I won't turn Tom down if he wants me for his leading lady. But future forecasting never works—it's about as unreliable as those weather reports on the news. If there's one thing I've learned, it's that life is anything *but* predictable.

Here's how I see it: Life is like this wild and crazy roller-coaster ride, with lots of bumps and loops and hairpin turns. It takes your breath away; it scares you; it makes you want to scream and laugh out loud (sometimes even throw up). Once in a while, you catch a glimpse of a steep drop ahead on the tracks; other times, you're so busy enjoying the view as you climb higher and higher, you never notice it coming. I'm not sure which is better: to know you are about to plummet (and dread it), or to just close your eyes, hold on tight, and let momentum carry you. I think I'd choose the latter. Otherwise, where's the thrill?

I don't know what my future holds; I won't even try to guess (I'm also afraid I'll jinx myself!). But here is what I *do* know: There will be good times and bad times and plenty of twists and turns on my ride. I know for sure that they'll be there, I just don't know where or when or how many. Some people lead charmed lives—everything always seems to go their way—then out of the blue, something unexpected happens and they're totally unprepared for it. For that reason, I'm glad I've been through so much, so young. I now know I can handle anything that comes my way. So instead of predicting my future, I think I'd rather share with you my wish list:

- I hope my future will include me becoming a wife and a mom. A *good* mom. My grandma and my mother have set great examples, and they're tough acts to follow, but I'll give it my best shot.

- I'd love to star on Broadway and to continue acting on TV and in the movies. You should always do what you love.

- I'd like to make another record—this time, my way.

- I hope that I'm a leader rather than a follower, someone who stands up for what she believes even if it's not the most popular view. And I pray I have the courage to do it!

- I hope that I never lose sight of what really matters in life: my family, my friends, my health. Notice this list did not include "cute shoes from Prada." Material things are great. Don't get me wrong, I can always shop and do some serious damage. But sometimes I have to remind myself, "Jamie, all this stuff is just that—*stuff.*" Keep it in perspective and don't ever let dollar signs make your decisions for you.

- I'd like to make a difference the world in some small way (or some not-so-small way!)—to touch people, move people, maybe even save people.

That last one is my greatest wish, the reason I wrote this book, the reason I think my life has taken the strange twists and turns that it has so far. I have to believe that, because I have seen time and time again how fate steps in and gives you a push. It puts you at some place, at some time with all the right choices in front of you—you just have to make them.

For this reason, I will never forget Miami. It was two years ago in November. I was with my mom, and I had a performance in Fort Meyers, so we decided to drive to South Beach, just us girls, for two days of fun in the sun. We checked into a nice hotel very early in the morning, like 3 or 4 A.M. (we had been driving all night). We were exhausted, and had just drifted off to sleep when I heard this horrible sound next door that made the hair on the back of my neck stand on end. It sounded like a child screaming or throwing a tantrum. I bolted up in bed and listened for about ten seconds: "No! Stop! Let go of me! I don't want to! You're hurting me! You're going to kill me!" Horrified, I realized that what I was hearing was a young woman being raped.

I jumped out of bed and raced next door. "Jamie!" my mother screamed after me. "What are you doing? Come back!" I saw the door to the other room was slightly ajar and a hand was trying to pry it open further. There were people just standing there in the hall, not doing anything. Not calling the police, not trying to save her. *Nothing.* I didn't think; I just acted. I kicked the door open (a real *Charlie's Angels* maneuver) and I grabbed the girl and ran with her into my room. We locked the door behind us and called hotel security.

All I could think was that she looked like an angel. She was a teenager, a tiny, petite girl with blonde hair and these big blue eyes. She clung to me, crying and shaking. "What does he look like?" I asked her. She said, between sobs, "His name is James, he has an English accent, he's wearing a T-shirt, and he has a cut over his eye." We called downstairs, described him, and said, "Don't let this guy leave!" Then, she told us what had happened. She was a runaway, and he and his friend met her and said they worked on a cruise ship and could get her a job. They took her upstairs to their hotel room, ordered tons of room service and champagne, and watched TV. Then the friend left, and James started to massage her shoulders. When she told him to stop, he jumped on top of her, and when she tried to put up a fight, he put a pillow over her face and tried to suffocate her. She was able to reach the bottle of water on the room service cart and cracked it over his head. She made it toward the door just as I burst in.

"I don't understand, he was so nice, he was so nice," she cried in my arms. The police and the FBI came and questioned us all about what went on. Of course, the creep denied everything; he actually didn't even try to leave the hotel. He said she had come on to him. I was furious. "Can't you see she's terrified? Why would she lie?" I screamed at the officers. "He's the liar. How can you believe him? He was trying to kill her—we heard the screams." She even had marks on her neck from where he had tried to strangle her.

Later, we learned that this guy had a record; he had several passports, wasn't British or working on a cruise ship, and was wanted in several states. I gave a deposition, and because of this, he plead guilty without the case ever going to trial. So I have the satisfaction of knowing I helped put this disgusting dirtbag behind bars where he can't hurt anyone else for a long time.

After the police and everyone left, I was very shaken up and I called all my girlfriends. "Can you believe those times on spring break or at clubs when we would go hang out with some cute guys we met?" I told them. "What if this had happened to one of us?" You always hear about these things, but you never think it could happen to you. What if I was the one screaming for help and nobody helped me? To this day, every time I hear a noise when I'm in a hotel room I jump a mile. I will never, *ever* forget this, especially what happened the next night.

It was midnight, and my mom and I were trying to get some rest, when there was a knock at our door (yup, we jumped a mile). It was the girl, and she was all bundled up in a scarf and a jacket. "They told me you're some TV star, but I don't have a TV so I didn't know," she said softly. There were tears in her eyes. "I'm sorry, I wish I had money to buy you flowers or something. But I wanted to thank you for saving my life. You're my hero."

Nothing I could do in my life—no award, no rave review, no big fat paycheck, no starring role—could ever mean as much to me as that girl telling me I was her hero. Wouldn't it be awesome if we all thought, "When I grow up, I want to be someone's hero?" I'm not saying rush in to dangerous situations without thinking about your own safety (I got a lecture from Mom on this, believe me). I'm just saying it really doesn't matter how rich, thin, or famous you are. What matters is that you make your life matter. Follow your dreams, challenge the odds, defy your critics, champion a cause, sing out until your voice is heard!

And don't beat yourself up if it takes years to do this, not to mention a lot of practice and perseverance (a stubborn streak doesn't hurt either).

Hey, it took me a long time, but I finally wised up.

Meadow vs. Me

Meadow	Me
Supersmart: a know-it-all	Smart, but I don't know every SAT word!
Experiments with drugs	Would never do drugs; my health means too much to me
Likes to sing	Likes to sing
Is dramatic (sometimes overly)	Is dramatic (sometimes overly)
Hides her feelings from people	Sometimes I show my emotions too much
Very plain	Very girly
Likes a bad boy	Loves a great guy
Is just like her dad	Is just like her mom
Dad is a mob boss	Dad is a baseball league boss
Has one little brother	I have two big bros
Grew up in "Joisey"	Grew up in "Longisland"
Goes to college in NYC	Went to college for a semester in NYC
Always has an attitude	I always try to have a positive attitude!
She's Italian	I'm Jewban
Loves pasta	Loves black beans and rice
Makes mistakes	Makes mistakes . . . but learns from them

Afterword

Getting Involved

The other day I got this email from a girl I used to baby-sit. She's now thirteen, and she was writing to fill me in about school and friends and stuff. Then, right in the middle of the email, she says, "I'm so fat. I really hate myself." I didn't want to make a big deal out of it, but her next email said the same thing: "My friends and I were talking about dieting. I really need to lose weight." It was like a little cry for help. She knew what I had been through with my own eating disorder because I've been pretty open about it, and she was asking me—without actually asking me—to help. I wrote back, "If you need me, I'm here for you." Suddenly, she started pouring out her fears and her feelings. I've since talked to her older sister, who's a friend, and her family is helping her deal with her problem. I can't begin to tell you how great that makes me feel—to know that one less girl has to suffer in silence. She'll be okay.

I wanted to reach out to as many people as possible about my eating disorder, so I'm now working with the National Eating Disorders Association (NEDA). I am really honored, and I'm looking forward to being more than just a name for this organization. I want to be hands-on and meet as many kids and parents as possible. I want to spread the word. It's a tough battle, but it's one we can win.

Here's a good start. This chapter outlines the basics about eating disorders, what they are, how to recognize if someone you know has one (or maybe you do), and how to help. If any of these signs and symptoms sound familiar, please don't waste any time. Contact the National Eating Disorders Association or any of these organizations (See "Where to Turn for Help" on page 151). Tell a parent, a teacher, a trusted friend. Get help! Every minute counts because eating disorders can—and will—have tragic consequences if left untreated.

NEED NUMBERS?

- In the United States, 5 to 10 million girls and women and 1 million boys and men are struggling with eating disorders.

- Approximately one in every five girls will develop a full-blown eating disorder.

- In a single person's lifetime, approximately 50,000 individuals will die due to eating disorders.

Trust me, if you wise up, and you could actually save a life. Maybe even your own.

—*Jamie*

Who gets eating disorders?

Eating disorders affect 5 to 10 million American adolescent girls and women and approximately one million American boys and men. Eating disorders know no race, age, class, or gender. They can happen to anyone, to children as young as three years old and adults as old as ninety. However, the typical age of onset is twelve to eighteen years old.

143

What causes eating disorders?

While eating disorders may begin with preoccupations with food and weight, they are most often about much more than food. Doctors and researchers are still learning about the many emotional and psychological aspects that underlie them. We do know this: For some, dieting, bingeing, and purging may begin as a way to cope with painful emotions and to feel in control of one's life, but ultimately, these behaviors are self-destructive.

What are the different types of eating disorders?

The three most talked about eating disorders are anorexia nervosa (self-starvation), bulimia nervosa (binge-purge), and binge eating disorder (bingeing).

How do you know if someone you know (or you) has anorexia nervosa?

- She or he refuses to maintain body weight at or above a minimally normal weight for height, body type, age, and activity level

- Intense fear of weight gain or being "fat"

- Feels "fat" or overweight despite dramatic weight loss

- Loss of menstrual periods

- Extremely concerned with body weight and shape

What are the warning signs of anorexia?

- Dramatic weight loss

- Preoccupation with weight, food, calories, fat grams, and dieting

- Refusal to eat certain foods, progressing to restrictions against whole categories of food (i.e., no carbohydrates, etc.)

- Frequent comments about feeling "fat" or overweight despite weight loss

- Anxiety about gaining weight or being "fat"

- Denial of hunger

- Development of food rituals (i.e., eating foods in certain orders, excessive chewing, rearranging food on a plate)

- Consistent excuses to avoid mealtimes or situations involving food

- Excessive, rigid exercise regimen—despite weather, fatigue, illness, or injury, there is a need to "burn off" all calories taken in

- Withdrawal from usual friends and activities

- In general, behaviors and attitudes indicating that weight loss, dieting, and control of food are becoming primary concerns

What are the health consequences of anorexia?

Anorexia nervosa involves self-starvation. The body is denied the essential nutrients it needs to function normally, so it is forced to slow down all of its processes to conserve energy. This "slowing down" can have serious medical consequences:

- Abnormally slow heart rate and low blood pressure, which mean that the heart muscle is changing. The risk for heart failure rises as heart rate and blood pressure levels sink lower and lower

- Reduction of bone density (osteoporosis), which results in dry, brittle bones

- Muscle loss and weakness

- Severe dehydration, which can result in kidney failure

- Fainting, fatigue, and overall weakness

- Dry hair and skin; hair loss is common

- Growth of a downy layer of hair called "lanugo" all over the body, including the face, in an effort to keep the body warm

How do you know if someone (or you) has bulimia?

- She or he eats large quantities of food in short periods of time, often secretly, without regard to feelings of "hunger" or "fullness," and to the point of feeling "out of control" while eating

- Follows these "binges" with some form of purging or compensatory behavior to make up for the excessive calories taken in: self-induced vomiting, laxative or diuretic abuse, fasting, and/or obsessive or compulsive exercise

- Extremely concerned with body weight and shape

What are the warning signs of bulimia?

- Evidence of binge-eating, including disappearance of large amounts of food in short periods of time or the existence of wrappers and containers indicating the consumption of large amounts of food

- Evidence of purging behaviors, including frequent trips to the bathroom after meals, signs and/or smells of vomiting, presence of wrappers or packages of laxatives or diuretics

- Excessive, rigid exercise regimen—despite weather, fatigue, illness, or injury, the need to "burn off" calories taken in

- Unusual swelling of the cheeks or jaw area

- Calluses on the back of the hands and knuckles from self-induced vomiting

- Discoloration or staining of the teeth

- Creation of complex lifestyle schedules or rituals to make time for binge-and-purge sessions

- Withdrawal from usual friends and activities

- In general, behaviors and attitudes indicating that weight loss, dieting, and control of food are becoming primary concerns

What are the health consequences of bulimia?

Bulimia nervosa can be extremely harmful to the body. The recurrent binge-and-purge cycles can impact the entire digestive system and can lead to electrolyte and chemical imbalances in the body that affect the heart and other major organ function:

- Electrolyte imbalances that can lead to irregular heartbeats and possibly heart failure and death. Electrolyte imbalance is caused by dehydration and loss of potassium and sodium from the body as a result of purging behaviors

- Potential for gastric rupture during periods of bingeing. Inflammation and possible rupture of the esophagus from frequent vomiting

- Tooth decay and staining from stomach acids released during frequent vomiting

- Chronic irregular bowel movements and constipation as a result of laxative abuse

- Peptic ulcers and pancreatitis

How do you know if someone (or you) has binge eating disorder?

- She or he has frequent episodes of eating large quantities of food in short periods of time often secretly, without regard to feelings of "hunger" or "fullness"

- Frequently feels "out of control" during binges

- Eats large quantities of food rapidly, without really tasting the food

- Eats alone

- Feels shame, disgust, or guilt after a binge

What are the health consequences of binge eating disorder?

Binge eating disorder often results in some of the health risks associated with clinical obesity:

- High blood pressure

- High cholesterol levels

- Heart disease as a result of elevated triglyceride levels

- Secondary diabetes

- Gallbladder disease

WHERE TO TURN FOR HELP

Contact my group or any of these other excellent resources:

The National Eating Disorders Association (NEDA)
603 Stewart St., Suite 803
Seattle, WA 98101
(206) 382-3587
www.nationaleatingdisorders.org

American Anorexia Bulimia Association, Inc.
165 West 46th Street, Suite 1108
New York, NY 10036
(212) 575-6200
www.aabainc.org

Academy for Eating Disorders
6728 Old McLean Drive
McLean, VA 22101
(703) 556-9222
www.aedweb.org

Anorexia Nervosa and Related Eating Disorders, Inc.
P.O. Box 5102
Eugene, OR 97401
(503) 344-1144
www.anred.com

National Association of Anorexia Nervosa and
Associated Disorders
Box 7
Highland Park, IL 60036
(847) 831-3438
www.anad.org

The Alliance for Eating Disorders Awareness
P.O. Box 13155
North Palm Beach, FL 33408-3155
(561) 841-0900
www.eatingdisorderinfo.org

A wonderful group established by Johanna Kandel, a twenty-three-year-old former anorexic. Johanna came to visit me after a performance of *Cinderella,* and told me all about her organization. She's really dedicated to reaching young girls and spreading awareness.

Harvard Eating Disorders Center
WACC 725, 15 Parkman Street
Boston, MA 02114
(617) 236-7766
www.hedc.org

The International Association of Eating Disorders
Professionals
P.O. Box 35882
Phoenix, AZ 85069-8552
(602) 934-3024
www.iaedp.com

The National Eating Disorder Information
Centre (Canada)
CW 1-211,
200 Elizabeth Street
M5G 2C4
(416) 340-4156
www.nedic.ca

Toll-free help-lines. Call for doctor referrals in
your local area or for more information on eating
disorders.

National Eating Disorders Association
(800) 931-2237

The International Association of Eating Disorders
Professionals
(800) 800-8126

National Association of Anorexia Nervosa and
Associated Disorders
(847) 831-3438

The National Eating Disorders Information Centre
(866) 633-4220
Canada

1-800-THERAPIST
(800) 843-7274

What to do if you suspect someone has an eating disorder

You cannot force someone to seek help, change their habits, or adjust their attitudes. You will make important progress in honestly sharing your concerns, providing support, and knowing where to go for more information.

- *Learn* as much as you can about eating disorders. Read books, articles, and brochures.

- *Know the differences* between facts and myths about weight, nutrition, and exercise. Knowing the facts will help you reason against any inaccurate ideas that your friend may be using as excuses to maintain her disordered eating patterns.

- *Be honest.* Talk openly and honestly about your concerns with the person who is struggling with eating or body image problems. Avoiding it or ignoring it won't help!

- *Be caring, but be firm.* Caring about your friend does not mean being manipulated by her. Your friend must be responsible for her actions and their consequences. Avoid making "rules," promises, or expectations that you cannot or will not uphold. (For example, "I promise not to tell anyone," or, "If you do this one more time I'll never talk to you again.")

- *Tell someone.* It may seem difficult to know when, if at all, to tell someone else about your concerns. Addressing body image or eating problems in their beginning stages probably offers your friend the best chance for working through these issues and becoming healthy again. Don't wait until the situation is so severe that your friend's life is in danger. If you have already spoken with your friend and still feel like more steps need to be taken to address these issues, consider telling her parents, a teacher, a doctor, a counselor, a nutritionist, or any trusted adult. She needs as much support and understanding as possible from the people in her life.

What should I say to a friend who might have an eating disorder?

If you are worried about your friend's eating behaviors or attitudes, then you should express your concerns to her in a loving and supportive way. It is important to handle these issues with honesty and respect. It is also important to discuss your worries early on, rather than waiting until your friend has endured many of the damaging physical and emotional effects of eating disorders. In a private and relaxed setting, talk to your friend in a *calm* and *caring* way about the specific things you have seen or felt that have made you worry.

- *Share your memories* of two or three specific times when you felt concerned, afraid, or uneasy because of her eating rituals.

- *Talk about the feelings you experienced* as a result of these events.

- Try to do this in a very *supportive, nonconfrontational* way. Here are three suggestions:

1. *Use "I" statements.* For example: "I'm concerned about you because you refuse to eat breakfast or lunch." or "It makes me afraid to hear you vomiting."

2. *Avoid accusational "you" statements.* For example: "You have to eat something!" " You must be crazy!" or "You're out of control!"

3. *Avoid giving simple solutions.* For example: "If you'd just stop, everything would be fine!"

If your friend has become obsessed with eating, exercising, or dieting, she probably needs professional help. Your friend may be angry that you are questioning her attitudes and behaviors. Your friend may deny that there is a problem. If your friend won't listen to your concerns, you may need to tell someone else—someone who can help. Consider talking to your friend's parents, a teacher, a doctor, a counselor, a nutritionist, or any trusted adult. Your friend needs as much support and understanding as possible from the people in her life.

FOR PARENTS: 10 things you can do to prevent your kid from getting an eating disorder

1. Consider your thoughts, attitudes, and behaviors toward your own body and the way that these beliefs have been shaped by the forces of weight-ism and sexism. Then educate your children about (a) the genetic basis for the natural diversity of human body shapes and sizes, and (b) the nature and ugliness of prejudice.

2. Make an effort to maintain positive, healthy attitudes and behaviors. Children learn from the things you say and do! Avoid conveying an attitude which says in effect, "I will like you more if you lose weight, don't eat so much, look more like the slender models in ads, fit into smaller clothes,

etc." Decide what you can do and what you can stop doing to reduce the teasing, criticism, blaming, staring, etc. that reinforce the idea that larger or fatter is "bad" and smaller or thinner is "good."

3. Learn about and discuss with your daughters and sons (a) the dangers of trying to alter one's body shape through dieting, (b) the value of moderate exercise for health, and (c) the importance of eating a variety of foods in well-balanced meals consumed at least three times a day. Avoid categorizing foods into "good/safe/no-fat or low-fat" vs. "bad/dangerous/ fattening." Be a good role model in regard to sensible eating, exercise, and self-acceptance.

4. Make a commitment not to avoid activities (such as swimming, sunbathing, dancing, etc.) simply because they call attention to your weight and shape. Refuse to wear clothes that are uncomfortable or that you don't like but wear simply because they divert attention from your weight or shape.

5. Make a commitment to exercise for the joy of feeling your body move and grow stronger, not to purge fat from your body or to compensate for calories eaten.

158

6. Practice taking people seriously for what they say, feel, and do, not for how slender or "well put together" they appear.

7. Help children appreciate and resist the ways in which television, magazines, and other media distort the true diversity of human body types and imply that a slender body means power, excitement, popularity, or perfection.

8. Educate boys and girls about various forms of prejudice, including weightism, and help them understand their responsibilities for preventing them.

9. Encourage your children to be active and to enjoy what their bodies can do and feel like. Do not limit their caloric intake unless a physician requests that you do this because of a medical problem.

10. Do whatever you can to promote the self-esteem and self-respect of all of your children in intellectual, athletic, and social endeavors. Give boys and girls the same opportunities and encouragement. Be careful not to suggest that females are less important than males, e.g., by exempting males from housework or childcare. A well-rounded sense of self and solid self-esteem are perhaps the best antidotes to dieting and disordered eating.

A message from NEDA about Jamie

The board and staff of the National Eating Disorders Association have been so grateful for Jamie's participation in our efforts to eliminate eating disorders and body dissatisfaction. Jamie was selected as a spokesperson for our "Listen to Your Body" Campaign because she is a strong role model for girls. She also understands the dangers of dieting, and how a simple wish to lose a few pounds can snowball into a serious eating disorder. In her work with our organization, she speaks out at schools, at National Eating Disorders Association events, and in the media to help the public gain a better understanding of eating disorders and body image issues. Jamie clearly wants to help girls avoid the body image and eating problems that so strongly impacted her life. Girls know they can ask Jamie anything and she will respond with honesty and compassion. Most importantly, Jamie turns her interests and concerns into *action!* She is helping us create a world where self-esteem is not weighed in pounds on a scale.

—**Sue Yuzer, M.S.W.,**
    Executive Director,
    National Eating Disorders Association

From the National Eating Disorders Association:

A Declaration of Independence for a Weight-Obsessed World

I, the undersigned, do hereby declare that from this day forward, I will choose to live my life by the following tenets. In so doing, I declare myself free and independent from the pressures and constraints of a weight-obsessed world.

- I will accept my body in its natural shape and size.

- I will celebrate all that my body can do for me each day.

- I will treat my body with respect, giving it enough rest, fueling it with a variety of foods, exercising it moderately, and listening to what it needs.

- I will choose to resist our society's pressures to judge myself and other people on physical characteristics like body weight, shape, or size. I will respect people based on the qualities of their character and the impact of their accomplishments.

- I will refuse to deny my body of valuable nutrients by dieting or using weight loss products.

- I will avoid categorizing foods as either "good" or "bad." I will not associate guilt or shame with eating certain foods. Instead, I will nourish my body with a balance of foods, listening and responding to what it needs.

- I will not use food to mask my emotional needs.

- I will not avoid participating in activities that I enjoy (i.e., swimming, dancing, enjoying a meal) simply because I am self-conscious about the way my body looks. I will recognize that I have the right to enjoy any activities regardless of my body shape or size.

- I will believe that my self-esteem and identity come from within!

Signature_____Date_____

*Diagnostic and treatment Information in this chapter has been provided in part by the National Eating Disorders Association.